LATINOS IN MUSEUMS

IUPLR (Inter-University Program for Latino Research) working group agenda meeting. San Francisco 1993.

LATINOS IN MUSEUMS:
A Heritage Reclaimed

edited by

Antonio Ríos-Bustamante

and

Christine Marin

KRIEGER PUBLISHING COMPANY
MALABAR, FLORIDA
1998

Original Edition   1998

Printed and Published by
KRIEGER PUBLISHING COMPANY
KRIEGER DRIVE
MALABAR, FLORIDA 32950

Library of Congress Cataloging-in-Publication Data

Latinos in museums : a hertige reclaimed / edited by Antonio José
    Ríos–Bustamante and Christine Marin. — Original ed.
        p.   cm. — (Public history series)
    Includes bibliographical references (p.   ) and index.
    ISBN 0–89464–981–7 (hardcover : alk. paper)
    1. Hispanics Americans—Museums. 2. Hispanic Americans—
Intellectual life. I. Ríos-Bustamante, Antonio José. II. Marin,
Christine. III. Series.
  AM11.L38   1998
    305.86073—dc21   97–26230
                                                         CIP

10 9 8 7 6 5 4 3 2

The editors and contributors dedicate this book to
the memory of the late Sister Karen Boccalero,
founder of Self-Help Graphics

CONTENTS

ILLUSTRATIONS

ACKNOWLEDGMENTS

We wish to acknowledge the support provided by the Mexican American Studies and Research Center, University of Arizona; the editorial assistance of Virginia Croft; and the advice of Olga Yolanda Soto-Bernal which greatly enhanced this publication.

ABOUT THE AUTHORS

Antonio Ríos-Bustamante: Co-editor, associate professor of Mexican American history, University of Arizona, Tucson. Coordinator of Historical and Museum Programs. Producer of exhibits, "Images of Mexican Los Angeles, 1781-Present"; "The Latino Olympians, 1896–1984." Producer of video documentary, "Latino Hollywood, 1911–1940." Author, editor of over forty publications, including seven monographs and books.

Christine Marin: Co-editor, curator and archivist at the Chicano Research Collection, Hayden Library, Arizona State University, Tempe. Author of numerous publications and producer of "The Chicano Experience in Arizona."

Theresa Chavez: Playwright, producer, and assistant professor, Los Angeles, California. Descendent of Lugo family.

Karen Mary Davalos: Art historian, visiting scholar, Chicano Studies Program, Ethnic Studies Department, University of California, Berkeley.

Martha Gutierrez Steinkamp: Chairperson of the National Advisory Board Cuban Museum of the Americas; Museum consultant for Broward County School District; Southeast representative and vice chair of the Latino Network, American Association of Museums.

E. Liane Hernandez: Graduate student in art history, University of Arizona, Tucson.

Cynthia E. Orozco: Assistant professor of history, visiting scholar, Center for Regional Studies, University of New Mexico, Albuquerque. Former research associate, Institute of Texan Cultures. Author of numerous publications.

Reina Alejandra Prado Saldivar: Graduate student in art history, University of Arizona, Tucson.

INTRODUCTION

Prior to the early 1970s, Latino public history as an enterprise involving Latino scholars and community was nonexistent in American public history museums and agencies. It was as if all United States history programs were conducted by Canadian scholars and there were no American curators or historians involved in their development. Or as if African American and Native American historical programs were conducted entirely by non-African Americans and non-Native Americans. The few historical programs that touched on aspects of Latino history usually addressed other themes and failed to focus on the Latino peoples of the United States. The focus was often on elite colonial administrators rather than on Mexicans or Puerto Ricans, who were mentioned as objects rather than as central subjects.

The period since 1970 has witnessed the development of Latino public history and art movements directed by Latino professionals. Latino public history and public art share many common concerns regarding the interpretation of Latino culture. Their concerns frequently overlap and converge, as in the case of the Chicano Art, Resistance and Affirmation (CARA) exhibition. They may also have different emphasis on either the aesthetic or the historical dimension.

Unlike African American public history and art programs, which developed from the intellectual and institutional milieu of African American universities and colleges, Latino public history and art programs have developed at different rates. Latino public history programs have had a slower start, which has been reflected in their organization and in public and professional awareness. In part the difference is due to the dynamism of Latino artists as applied practitioners of Chicano, Puerto Rican, and Latino art. Within the arts, Latino artists have led and scholars followed, whereas in history, applied history has not been encouraged in the training of most Latino historians.

Until recently there was a gap between academic historians in the United States and community historians such as genealogists, curators, and nondegreed community historians. In addition, there have been few history curators, museum directors, and professionals working on U.S. Latino history. Those few Latino curators have rarely had the seniority to set work agendas emphasizing Latino history and culture.

In American museums Latino history has often suffered decontextualization and content neutering in much the same way as Latino art, designed to sanitize it and make it fit outdated stereotypes such as the "Spanish myth heritage." (See Chapter 3.) Another potential danger has been nationalistic simplification, which can lead to the reproduction or creation of both old and new gender and national chauvinisms and the glorification of a stereotypical history. This includes the failure to adequately depict women's history and female perspectives or to recognize the complex multiracial, multicultural origins of Latinos (including Mexicans, Puerto Ricans, and others) outside and inside the United States.

Latinos in the United States are diverse, comprising several major groups and many smaller ones. Multiethnic and multicultural, the Latino heritage includes Native American, African, European, and Asian origins and traditions. Beginning with the Native American/European/African encounter resulting from Spanish, Portuguese, and other colonization, Latinos have continued to develop cultural exchanges. A complex array of native identities preceded the arrival of Europeans: Meshica, Chichimeca, Taino, Sinboney, and Caribe. Colonization and resistance resulted in new multiple identities: criollo, converso, indio, mestizo, mulatto. And the independence era introduced newly affirmed national identities: Mexicano, Colombiano, Cubano, Dominicano, Puertoriqueño.

Although all Latin American nationalities are represented today among United States Latinos, several groups have had a larger and longer demographic and historical presence. These are the Mexicans, Puerto Ricans, and Cubans. Other groups with a more recent historical but increasingly important demographic presence include the Dominicanos, Colombianos, Guatemaltecos, Salvadoreños, and Nicaraguenses.

Since the 1970 census adopted it, the term *Hispanic* has seen major use as an official and alternative unifying term to *Latino*. While unifying concepts such as Latino, Hispanic, Latin American, and Hispano Americano go back to the Pan Americanism of Bolívar and before that to the unifying force of Spanish colonization, the groups have strongly demarcated histories and identities. Mexicans are the largest Latino group, with over 60 percent of the population, and constitute a native population in the Southwest, where they descended from Spanish intermarriage with Indian peoples as well as migration from central Mexico. In 1848, as a result of the Mexican American War, 100,000 Mexicans became U.S. citizens after the Treaty of Guadalupe Hidalgo. Later, between 1900 and 1920 over one million Mexicans immigrated to the United States. Between 1940 and 1990 another 6 million immigrated. As a result of population growth and immigration there are more than 16 million Mexican Americans and Mexicans living in the United States today.

Puerto Ricans and Cubans have early antecedents in the southeastern United States. La Florida, which included most of the southern Gulf

Coast, was attached to the Captaincy General of Cuba and alternated between the Bishoprics of Cuba and Puerto Rico. Pre-twentieth-century migration of Cubans and Puerto Ricans was small, however, and confined to Florida and small urban communities in New York, New Orleans, and a few other coastal cities. Such communities also included Spaniards and a few Central and South Americans.

With the 1849 Gold Rush, northern California also attracted early Central and South American settlers, mainly Chilenos, Salvadoreños, and Guatemaltecos concentrated in San Francisco. Chicago, Detroit, New Orleans, and Miami also developed diverse Latino communities: Chicago, mainly Mexican, Puerto Rican, and Colombian; Washington, D.C., and New Orleans, mostly Central American and Colombian; and Miami, mainly Cubans, along with Central Americans, Puerto Ricans, and Mexicans. New York City has probably the most diverse community, predominantly Puerto Rican and Dominican, with other Latinos from every country in Latin America. Most major Latino communities are becoming increasingly diverse due to new Latin American immigration and the migration of Mexicans to the East Coast and South and Puerto Ricans to the West Coast and Southwest.

Issues of national, regional, and overall identity are important and controversial for all Latino groups. Most prefer to identify themselves primarily by their core national or regional identity and only secondarily by one of the broad terms such as Latino or Hispanic. Organizations and programs generally reflect this identification, as in, for example, the Museo Cubano in Miami or the Mexican Fine Arts Center Museum in Chicago. In principle, both types of identity are possible and will coexist: national or regional (Mexican, Puerto Rican, Cuban) and Latino or Hispanic. It is probably realistic and fair to say that both can be valid when they correspond to the needs and reality within particular Latino communities. For example, in Chicago there is no reason why there should not be both Mexican and Puerto Ricans museums and every reason why there should be. The only limitations or opportunities are those that exist or can be developed in particular communities.

At the national level there already exists the basis for networking and cooperation through the National Association of Latino Arts and Culture (NALAC), the directors of the Latino museums, the American Association of Museums (AAM), and the auspices of the Smithsonian Institution. This can and must be strengthened in ways that allow for national and regional diversity while facilitating collective policy formation at the national level in associations, institutions, and policy forums.

Latinos in the United States are further diversifying and adding to their heterogeneous origins, their centuries-old cultural and ethnic mestizaje. Latinos are intermarrying and developing multicultural relations with all other American ethnic and cultural groups, including Native Americans, African Americans, Asian Americans, Jewish Americans, and all Anglo-American ethnic groups. Mexicans, Puerto Ricans, and Cubans who already have Asian, African, or Jewish ancestry are further enriching their multicultural, multiethnic identity. Similarly, Latino Americans, like all other groups, have developed international connections through work, the military, business, education, and tourism. Some Mexican Americans, Puerto Ricans, and Cuban Americans now live in Japan, Germany, France, England, Spain, Argentina, India, Korea, and Saudi Arabia. Thus, U.S. Latinos are also an international people making contributions on a global scale.

This anthology originated with the Inter-University Program for Latino Research (IUPLR) Latinos in Museums Working Group based at the University of Arizona and Arizona State University. In December 1993 a planning meeting of the IUPLR Latinos in Museums Working Group was held at the Mexican Museum in San Francisco to develop a research agenda. This anthology is designed to provide an introduction to major themes and issues concerning Latino public history in the United States.

Among these concerns are the development of Latino public history programs; case studies of Latino museums; analysis of regional similarities and differences; review of Latino experience in museum training seminars; survey of the organization of national Latino arts and cultural coalitions; analysis of Latino representation in museums; and case studies of educational and cultural programs. The contributors include public history and art historians, teachers, and museum consultants who are actively involved in Latino public history and with American museums.

In "Latino Public History Programs, 1970s–1990s," Antonio Ríos-Bustamante provides a critical survey of the history of Latino public history programs. The chapter by Martha Gutierrez-Steinkamp, "Diversity Within Diversity: Latinos of South Florida," developed from a report made at the 1994 conference of the American Association of Museums regarding regional museum situations. The chapters by Karen Mary Davalos, "Exhibiting Mestizaje: The Poetics and Experience of the Mexican Fine Arts Center Museum," and Antonio Ríos-Bustamante, "The Hijacking of a Heritage: The California Museum of Latino History—Discourse, Politics, and History," are case studies of Latino museums.

E. Liane Hernandez, in "The National Latino Graduate Training Seminar," discusses the experience of participants in the Smithsonian's museum training workshop. Cynthia E. Orozco examines the development of programs in a report to the National Association of Latino Arts and

Culture (NALAC) in her chapter "Chicano and Latino Art and Culture Institutions in the Southwest: The Politics of Space, Race, and Money." Theresa Chavez, in "Public History and Performance: *L.A. Real*," demonstrates the importance of performance for interpreting history.

Reina Alejandra Prado Saldivar, in "Más Production of Art for the Masses: Serigraphs of Self-Help Graphic Arts, Inc.," presents the question of "how a community art center takes agency in defining itself, its role, and its production through a specific program," a study of the experience of Self-Help Graphics. In the chapter "Summary of the 1991–1992 National Survey of Latino and Native American Professional Museum Personnel," Antonio Ríos-Bustamante discusses the results of a national survey of museum professional representation.

In the 1990s important strides are being made by Latino public history and museum professionals: they have a greater presence in the established museums; they are working for the creation of Latino museums; and they are networking in national museum organizations, as in the formation of a Latino network within the American Association of Museums at the 1992 annual meeting. The AAM caucus was established through the initiative of Latino museum professionals in the Smithsonian Institution museums.

Another national cultural organization with important ramifications for national Latino museum policies and for the study of Latino museums is the National Association of Latino Arts and Culture, which was formed in September 1992 at a national conference in San Antonio, Texas. NALAC aims to influence national arts and cultural policies affecting Latinos in arts programs and museums.

Among the existing Latino museums, outstanding examples of success are the Mexican Fine Arts Center Museum of Chicago, the Mexican Museum in San Francisco, and the Museo del Barrio in New York. In 1995 the Mexican Fine Arts Center Museum was the recipient of the National Museum Service Award. That museum and the Mexican Museum are discussed in greater detail in the final essay of this book. Recently established Latino museums include the Mexic-Arte Museum in Austin, Texas; the Museo Chicano in Phoenix, Arizona; and the Museo de las Americas in Denver, Colorado.

The development and growth of new Latino museums, the organization of a Latino Task Force in the Smithsonian Institution, and the AAM Latino Museum Network indicate the need for new comprehensive studies of the Latino museum public; the development of independent Latino museums; and Latino representation in American museums. This anthology is dedicated to the reclamation of the Latino heritage and its representation in public history programs and museums.

1 LATINO PUBLIC HISTORY PROGRAMS, 1970s–1990s

Antonio Ríos-Bustamante

In a critical survey spanning more than two decades, Antonio Ríos-Bustamante examines the development and status of Latino applied history programs from the 1970s to the present. Several types of programs are reviewed, including those of the Smithsonian Institution and other historical museums. The author also surveys the development of Mexican American historical exhibitions and takes a look at interactive programs such as the San Diego-Tijuana History Fair. The essay concludes with a discussion of family history, genealogy, and oral history programs.

—The editors

Before examining the development and status of Latino applied history programs for the past twenty-five years, it is necessary to clarify the terms *public* and *applied history* to prevent confusion regarding their meaning. Public history is viewed by most public historians as applied history, with a historical product being created that has an impact in society outside the university.[1] It contrasts with purely academic historical research, which is the traditional domain of the university historian who publishes mainly in journals read by other scholars. Public history, as defined by public historians, also encompasses what has been called local or popular history, which includes history museums, historical societies and their public programs, and other types of public historical programs.[2]

Nonhistorians and other types of historians frequently have the impression that public history is primarily institutional, that it is the history of government agencies or large corporations. Applied local, regional, and ethnic historical programs are as much a part of public history as studies of government. Further, that portion of public history that emphasizes applied regional, ethnic, and local history programs has been steadily increasing during the last twenty years.[3]

The portion of public history activities that seriously addresses the his-

tory and culture of Mexican Americans and Latinos, particularly that
produced by those groups, is the primary focus of this essay. To date,
most public history programs funded by museums, historical societies,
and government agencies and conducted by professional historians and
other social scientists from their staffs have not been Latino-produced
programs. This continues to be so, for the simple reason that most history museums still have no Latino curators on their staffs. The Natural
History Museum of Los Angeles County, for example, the third largest
in the nation, has never had a Mexican American or Latino curator.[4]

Historical programs about the history of the Mexican community do
not, of course, have to be produced by Mexican Americans or other Latinos. Several major historical programs concerning the heritage of Mexican Americans have been curated and directed by Anglo-Americans, and
some have employed Latinos as supporting staff or volunteers. One of
the best of these programs was "American Encounters," which the Smithsonian Institution produced to mark the quincentenary year of 1992.
Directed and co-curated by Lonn Taylor, it examines the interaction
of American Indians, Hispanics, and Anglo-Americans in New Mexico
over five centuries.[5] Other outstanding programs produced with little or
no Latino participation include the Smithsonian Institution Traveling
Exhibition Service's "Africa's Legacy in Mexico: Photographs by Tony
Gleaton"[6] and the Smithsonian's largest quincentenary year exhibition,
the National Museum of Natural History's "Seeds of Change," directed
by Carolyn Margolis and coordinated by Herman J. Viola. "Seeds of
Change" treated the encounter on a massive scale and employed scholarly consultants, but had no U.S. Latino curators and limited participation by U.S. Latino scholars.[7]

Other examples include "The Mexican Texans," produced by the Institute of Texan Cultures at the University of Texas, Austin, which Samuel
P. Nesmith curated in 1981; "Tucson from Rancho to Barrio," produced
by the Arizona Historical Society and curated by Thomas Sheridan; and
more recently, "Familia y Fe," directed by Dr. William Wroth and Dr.
Helen Lucero, which was exhibited in the new Hispanic Heritage wing
of the Museum of International Folk Art in Santa Fe, New Mexico.[8]

Latino scholars are the first to acknowledge the important contributions of Anglo scholars in the study and preservation of Latino history.
Their important contributions, however, cannot substitute for the training and recruitment of Latino museum professionals. Nor can it fulfill
the tremendous work of public education that awaits future generations
of Mexican American and Latino scholars and their colleagues of all ethnic and cultural groups.[9]

LATINO APPLIED HISTORY PROGRAMS

The new applied history must start with the premise of equal respect for all people of all ethnic, cultural, and gender groups. It is the responsibility of Latino scholars to document their historical and cultural contributions with the greatest regard for and recognition of the interdependency of all peoples. Latino and Mexican American public history must not ape the ethnocentric gender and racial chauvinism of past dominant culture scholarly paradigms. Latino applied history must actively seek wide public exposure. It must not remain a mystery that is relegated to a tomblike environment for a necrophilic elite.

The mission of the new Latino/Mexican American historians is to take this history to the community, especially to Mexican elementary and secondary school youth. Despite the hard-won achievements of Mexican American historians, anthropologists, and other scholars over the last three decades, the results of their research have hardly begun to enter the public schools. Not even 5 percent of Mexican American elementary school students have ever taken a course in Mexican American history or even one in which it is a significant component. These young people still receive from their education the implicit and sometimes still overt message that Mexicans, Mexican Americans, and Latinos have contributed little or nothing to this society. Such a message contributes to the creation and reinforcement of a false and negative image. This image is also conveyed to young people of other ethnic groups and implicitly reinforces the idea that Latinos are a people without a history in this country and that Mexican Americans are "aliens" of little intellectual ability who should be grateful merely to breathe this nation's air.

Mexican American and Latino public history programs have challenged these stereotypes through documentation of the historical contributions of Mexicans to the United States and the world. Obviously, these programs are not the only efforts Latinos have made to document our history. Mexican American film and television professionals, in association with academic historians and social scientists, have led the way in producing video and film programs on historical subjects. The following discussion does not include public television historical programs because they have usually originated outside the public history sector.[10] Of course, film programs alone cannot fully document or educate people about the history of Mexicans and other Latinos in the United States.

Similarly, the following discussion does not emphasize public history programs that focus exclusively on Mexican or Latin American history and culture within the present territory of Mexico or Latin America unless they examine the contributions of Mexican Americans and Latinos in the United States.[11] The reason for not examining these programs is that treatment of Mexican or Latin American history without an examination of the history of Mexicans and Latinos in the United States conveys the idea that we have no history in this country. It also reinforces the false idea that Mexicans and Latinos in the United States have contributed little or nothing to either Latin America or the United States.

The focus herein is upon the efforts that Mexican Americans have made over the last two decades to create Mexican American and Latino public history programs where none have existed. This will be done through the examination of several types of successful public programs or activities produced by Mexican Americans during the 1980s. These programs include multimedia exhibitions that displayed photographs; presentations of artifacts with a narrative text; historical site surveys; the commemoration of community people who have been participants in historical events; and a border history fair.

Public art programs are mentioned when they include a major historical or archival dimension. Latino public art programs have received relatively more support than public history programs and are more advanced. For this reason, Latino public art programs require their own treatment.[12]

The production of historical exhibitions, both permanent and traveling, has been important because they are major media utilized by museums and historical societies that either are public institutions or receive major public funding. Mexican American and Latino taxpayers pay an increasing share of the support costs of these institutions, yet they receive little positive benefit compared to dominant ethnic-social groups.

THE CALIFORNIA HISPANIC
HISTORIC SITE SURVEY (1980)

Historic sites as a traditional dimension of public history continue to be of great importance to the development of Latino history programs. An important aspect of traditional public history has been the identification, interpretation, and preservation of national, state, and local historic sites. Because of five centuries of Latino historical presence within the territory of the United States, there are tremendous numbers of both official and unrecognized Latino historic sites in the nation. The best-known officially recognized sites are those associated with either Spanish colonization or the United States westward movement. Typically, until recent times the interpretation of these sites reflected an institutional and Eurocentric cultural bias that in many cases denied, minimized, or distorted the history of Mexican Americans. The working assumption in the recent past was that Mexican Americans were an alien immigrant group with little or no connection to the pre-1900 period, much less to that prior to 1848. A widespread view among curators, agency officials, and others concerned with sites was that the descendants of early Spanish-speaking settlers in the Southwest had almost entirely assimilated into the Anglo-American population. The history of the contemporary Mexican American community was viewed as having slight significance and few, if any, recognizable historic site associations.

During the last twenty years, this situation has improved slightly. Better trained and culturally sophisticated curators and agency personnel have developed better site interpretations, which are beginning to recognize the lengthy history and multiculturally diverse nature of Mexican Americans. For example, the interpretation at the Coronado National Movement outside Bernalillo, New Mexico, contains a mural and commentary that depict the extensive presence of Mexican Indian allies—the "*españoles Mexicans*" and mestizos who often formed the majority of the colonizing *entradas* (expeditions) into the north. Indian *capitanes de guerra* (war captains) and their *gente* (people/followers) are depicted alongside the European Spaniards.

In California the Department of Parks and Recreation is responsible for the identification, preservation, and interpretation of state historic sites. Among its duties is the administration of several historic parks with Hispanic themes, such as Old Town in San Diego and San Juan Bautista and, until recently El Pueblo de Los Angeles State Historic Park.[13]

Until the early 1970s, however, the department placed little emphasis upon serving California's Mexican American population and other ethnic populations. At the end of the 1970s, because of pressure from African Americans, Asian Americans, Mexican Americans, and culturally sensitive Anglo-Americans, the California State Legislature took action requiring the Department of Parks and Recreation to improve minority-group cultural representation in its programs.[14] The department responded to this pressure in part by developing several projects to enhance its service to California's ethnic groups, including Mexican Americans.

One of these projects was the "Interpretative Handbook of California Ethnic Groups" which the department was to use in the interpretation of California historic sites and parks. It was developed under the editorship of Dr. Carroll Purcell, public historian of the University of California, Santa Barbara, but was left unpublished when the liberal governorship of Jerry Brown was followed by the conservative one of George Deukmejian.

Another project was an ethnic historic sites survey of previously unrecognized sites of significance. In 1980 the Department of Parks and Recreation contracted with Mexican American historian Dr. Jose Pitti to coordinate the Mexican American component of the survey. Antonia Castañeda conducted the actual site survey, which included an extensive description of each site, while Dr. Carlos Cortes participated by writing an accompanying interpretive essay on Mexican American history in California.[15]

Castañeda conducted an extensive survey in which she contacted leading Mexican American historians, scholars, and community members throughout the state of California. She made a major effort to reflect all periods of the community's history and the participation of Mexicanas in shaping the history. Publication of the results of the survey was delayed until 1988, however, because of the more conservative political climate prevailing in the state.

The survey finally appeared in the department's publication *Five Views*, listing a total of ninety-nine sites surveyed.[16] Thirty of the site descriptions are published in the book. These California Hispanic historical sites span the entire period of the state's Mexican history and include all geographic areas of significance. Representative sites include the Sociedad Católica Regional Guadalupana (Guadalupana Hall) in Richmond, Contra Costa County; KGST radio station, Fresno County; the offices of *La Opinion* newspaper, Los Angeles; *Regeneración* newspaper offices, Los Angeles; and Chicano Park-Logan Heights, San Diego. The survey also assesses the potential for either preservation or damage to the sites. The California Hispanic historic survey is an important example of how Latino public historians can begin the process of ensuring that Mexican American historic sites will be effectively and equally preserved and interpreted for the public in the future.

MULTIMEDIA HISTORICAL EXHIBITIONS

The mainstays of historical museums are their permanent collections, permanent exhibitions, and major temporary and or traveling exhibitions. When people think of historical museums, they usually think of exhibitions. There are, however, few museums that contain a major exhibit on any aspect of Mexican American history; in fact, Mexican American history is not even considered to be part of their mission. Awareness of Mexican Americans in most United States historical museums can be compared to that of universities in the 1950s. How could it be otherwise when these institutions are staffed primarily by Anglos at the professional level?

Obviously, southwestern state museums include treatment of the Spanish and Mexican periods in their historical exhibitions. With few exceptions, however, these exhibits treat Mexicans as objects only to be mentioned when encountered by white men. Historical interpretation typically reflects a forty-year-old Borderlands school perspective. There is virtually no continuity of treatment of Mexicans into the late nineteenth and twentieth centuries. Implicitly, the view conveyed to visitors is that nineteenth-century Mexicans all assimilated and that the present Mexican community is composed of immigrant workers with no history. This, of course, is contradicted by the last twenty years of research in Mexican American history and culture by both Mexican American and Anglo scholars.

The development of Mexican American and Latino historical exhibitions and public history programs has been a difficult and uneven process. The public history establishment has provided little, if any, support for such programs. Major historical museums continue to make virtually no effort to employ Mexican American historians and social scientists. At least in the 1950s they had the excuse, lame even then, that there were no qualified Mexican American professionals to fill these positions. By the beginning of the 1990s, however, there was no longer any excuse for failure to expand both curatorial staffs and exhibition programs.

A handful of Mexican American scholars and community members have struggled against a mountain of inertia to research, plan, produce, curate, and present museum-quality historical programs on Mexican American history to the community and the general public.[17] While institutions have provided little support for such programs, encouragement and support have come at times from museum curators and other professional staff. Unfortunately, museum and agency staff who sympathize with or support Latino public history exhibitions are seldom in decision-making positions. Those having control over museum purse strings are, as individuals, generally the least likely to consider Mexican American history worthy of support.

In the absence of financial support for Latino public history programs from museums, Latino exhibition producers have successfully (and unsuccessfully) sought support from Mexican American studies programs, libraries, the National Endowment for the Humanities, state humanities councils, community college districts, school districts, private foundations, and corporations. The quality and popularity of large Latino public history exhibitions during the 1980s clearly demonstrated the tremendous need among Latinos, especially Mexican American youth, for such programs on a regular and continuous basis. It is clear, however, that the establishment of large ongoing Latino public history programs will require either public and private support for Latino historical museums or a drastic change in priorities within existing public historical museums.

"The Social and Cultural History of the Los Angeles Mexican Community"

In the following pages I will describe four successful Mexican American multimedia historical exhibitions of the 1980s. The first of these, "The Social and Cultural History of the Los Angeles Mexican Community, 1781–1981," was produced at the time of the Los Angeles Bicentennial celebration of the founding of Los Angeles.[18] Impetus for the project came from the disturbing realization that while exhibitions commemorating the heritage and contributions of several other ethnic groups to Los Angeles were planned, there was no such exhibition planned to commemorate the city's Mexican heritage.

The exhibition was conceived and produced by Antonio Ríos-Bustamante, Salvador Martinez, and Ernesto Collosi at the Mexican American Studies and Research Center at the University of California, Los Angeles, and directed by Dr. Juan Gomez-Quiñones. It received important cooperation from the Los Angeles County Museum of Natural History, the Huntington Library, and the Bancroft Library, which allowed the reproduction of visuals from their collections. William M. Mason, history curator at the Los Angeles County Museum of Natural History, participated as a co-principal investigator in the research phase, and an advisory council of nationally recognized Mexican American historians functioned as a review board and provided consultation in specific subject areas.

Support for the initial development of the project came from the Chicano Studies Research Center of the Los Angeles Community College District and private donors. The exhibition depicted the 200-year history of the Los Angeles Mexican community through photographs and a narrative text illustrating the themes of community, work, family, culture, and relations with other groups, including Indians, African Americans, and Anglo-Americans. The exhibit comprised 110 four-by eight-foot panels and photographic enlargements, accompanied by a bilingual narrative text in Spanish and English. Between September 1981 and 1984, it was shown at four major sites in southern California and at Rutgers University in New Jersey for a conference on Latino culture.

The California exhibition sites included East Los Angeles College; the John Wooden Center, University of California, Los Angeles; the Los Angeles County College District Administrative Offices' Plaza de la Raza; and California State University, Dominguez Hills. It is estimated that in excess of 200,000 visitors viewed the exhibit at these sites, with about 80 percent of the visitors being Mexican Americans. It is further estimated that at least one million other people read or heard about the exhibition through the media. Numerous articles were published, numerous media announcements made in both the English-and Spanish-language media. When the California Museum of Latino History was established in 1984, it acquired the rights to further develop and expand this exhibition for the future.

In 1995 the exhibit was renovated and expanded under the new name "Images of Mexican Los Angeles, 1781–1995." The exhibition curated by Ríos-Bustamante and Estrada, was displayed on the bottom floor of the historic Pico House located at El Pueblo de Los Angeles Historic Monument. The exhibition ran from September 15 to October 14, 1994. A little theater automatically replayed the thirty-minute video documentary, "Images of Mexican Los Angeles"/"Imagenes de Los Angeles Mexicano," in English and Spanish versions. The exhibition recorded an attendance of more than 10,000 persons.

"Two Centuries of Hispanic Theatre in the Southwest"

A significant prototype for historical cultural exhibitions dealing with dramatic and literary genres, "Two Centuries of Hispanic Theatre in the Southwest: A Multi-Media Exhibition" was conceived and produced by Dr. Nicolas Kanellos, University of Houston, as a result of many years of scholarly research for his dissertation and numerous other publications.[19] In a multimedia approach, the exhibit used visuals, artifacts, a narrative text, and public programs to depict the development and genres of Spanish-language theater among Mexicans in the Southwest. It also demonstrated the artistic and intellectual connections that linked the Mexican communities of the Southwest with Mexico and the Spanish-speaking world.

"Two Centuries of Hispanic Theatre" was the first large-scale historical exhibition produced by Mexican American scholars to receive funding from the National Endowment for the Humanities (NEH). The NEH had previously funded exhibitions with Hispanic themes, but these were produced and directed by Anglo-American scholars. This exhibition was an important breakthrough for Mexican American and Latino public history because it marked official recognition for the first time that Mexican American scholars could produce museum-quality historical programs.

It was also the first historical exhibition produced by Mexican Americans to tour extensively to multiple sites as part of a single national tour. From February through August 1982, the exhibition toured seven sites:

Houston Public Library, February 5–26; the Institute of Texan Cultures (San Antonio), March 7–26; El Paso Centennial Museum, April 3–30; Albuquerque Museum, May 14–31; Arizona Historical Society (Tucson), June 5–30; California State University at Los Angeles, July 10–30; and the Mexican Museum (San Francisco), August 7–27, 1982. Managed by project coordinator Francisco Blasco, the tour reached several hundred thousand viewers in seven cities and more than a million persons through media coverage. Later a booklet was published documenting the content of the exhibition. "Two Centuries of Hispanic Theatre in the Southwest" remains an outstanding model for Latino public history exhibitions.

"The Latino Olympians"

The largest and most ambitious Mexican American/Latino multimedia exhibition to date is "The Latino Olympians: A History of Latino American Participation in the Olympic Games, 1896 to Present."[20] The concept for the exhibit was developed by Antonio Ríos-Bustamante and William D. Estrada in 1982, and the design concept was by Ernesto Collosi. The development of the Latino Olympians exhibit was a direct outgrowth of the success of the 1981 exhibition on "The Social and Cultural History of the Los Angeles Mexican Community," which demonstrated the tremendous need of the Mexican American community for positive information about its historical contributions to the United States.

The producers had been deeply moved by the strong positive effects of the earlier exhibit upon elementary and secondary schoolchildren. In a particularly moving incident, one of the producers overheard a young Mexican American boy delightedly exclaiming to a friend, "That's my brother," upon seeing a man whose picture was on display in the large photographic panel in front of him. In reality the man was the nineteenth-century Los Angeles newspaper editor and postmaster Francisco Ramirez. Other incidents involved senior citizens discovering aunts or uncles in photographs such as the 1931 photo of a formal ball held by the mutualist organization Alianza Hispano Americana.

The 1984 Los Angeles Olympic Games appeared to the producers to offer a unique opportunity to research and create a large-scale exhibition depicting Latin American participation in the Olympic movement. Preliminary research revealed an extensive history of Latin American and United States Latino, including Mexican, participation in the games. The 1984 Olympics would be a unique international, cultural, and civic event that would affect the entire Los Angeles community. As early as 1982, lengthy newspaper articles described the Olympic organizers' concern that the African American and Mexican American communities would be alienated from the games because of the widespread economic deprivation in these communities.

A related, although usually understated, concern of Los Angeles civic leaders was that the impoverished inner-city barrios and ghettos would prove an eyesore that would alienate affluent visitors to the games. The Los Angeles Olympic Organizing Committee (LAOOC) expressed its intention to develop community projects that would involve African American and Latino youth and their communities in Olympic sports.

The producers of the Latino Olympians exhibit realized the intentions of the Olympic Organizing Committee, and the special nature of the event created unique opportunities to fund and produce a large-scale Latino multimedia exhibition. The greatest obstacle to achieving funding was general ignorance of the history of Latino participation in the games. The first reaction of potential funders, including representatives of the LAOOC, was that Latinos, especially Mexican Americans, simply did not have enough achievements or a history long enough to be worth depicting. This attitude was gradually overcome thanks to the prior research showing a long history of Latin American amateur sports, Latino participation in the modern Olympic Games going back to their inception in 1896, and Mexican American participation on the U.S. Olympic team going back to 1924, when boxer José Salas won the silver medal for the United States at the Paris Olympic Games.

After a long and difficult process, the producers finally secured funding from the Los Angeles Olympic Organizing Committee and a partial matching grant from the California Council for the Humanities. The site of the exhibition was the large 10,000-square-foot ground floor of the Pico House, a partially restored 1869 hotel that had been built by Alta California's last Mexican governor, Pio Pico, as a civic statement. It was an especially appropriate site that Pico, an ardent sportsman, would probably have appreciated. The three-story house fronted on the Los Angeles historic placita (small plaza) and Olvera Street, where the city was founded in 1781.

Since structural reconstruction of the Pico House in the 1960s had left the main room with only a dirt floor, a temporary floor had to be constructed for the exhibition. The exhibit consisted of two hundred mounted visuals; six hundred trilingual text placards in English, Spanish, and Japanese; and two specially commissioned murals depicting the history of Latin American amateur sports. A total room and exhibit environment was designed which used the five Olympic colors of blue, yellow, black, green, and red. Sets of five to ten panels alternated in the Olympic colors, for a total of two hundred 4- by 8-foot panels.

The exhibit was organized into four subdivisions. The first, a history of amateur sports in Latin American civilization from pre-Columbian to modern times, was symbolized by two large decorative murals depicting this history and the lead photographic panel, on which the original Olympic rings (on the altar of Apollo on the island of Delphi) were juxtaposed with a Mayan disc from Chichén Itza depicting a ball player. The next section dealt with the history of the games and Latin American participation, Olympiad by Olympiad, from 1896 to the present. The third section depicted official Latino participation in the Olympic movement and in the 1984 Los Angeles Olympic Organizing Committee. Another section presented the Latino members of the United States 1984 Olympic team. Decorative sections honored outstanding Olympians of all nations, and a decorative centerpiece displayed the Olympic flag and the flags of the United States and Latin American nations.

The exhibit opened on July 26, 1984, in a gala event on the placita. The program was opened by well-known film star Eddy Olmos, the producers, political leaders, and community representatives from all walks of life. The official ribbon-cutting ceremony for the exhibit was performed by two leading Mexican American Olympians, José Salas, the 1924 silver medal winner at the Paris Olympics, and Catherine Machado Grey, figure skater on the 1956 U.S. winter Olympics team. Interestingly, both José Salas and Catherine Machado are descendants of the Mexican founders of Los Angeles. So much for the myth of lack of historical continuity, which has for so long denied the real historic achievements of Mexican Americans.

The Latino Olympians exhibition at the Pico House took place from July 26 to September 30, 1984, during the Los Angeles Olympic Games and was one of the official programs of the Los Angeles Olympic Organizing Committee Community Relations Program (see Figure 1.1). A second major component of the Latino Olympians Program was a twenty-seven-page history booklet entitled "The Latino Olympians: A History of Latin American Participation in the Olympic Games." Funded by the LAOOC alone, the booklet was published in an edition of 50,000 copies and distributed free of charge to students in the Los Angeles Unified School District and Los Angeles schools.

The exhibition was viewed as an outstanding success and completely fulfilled its objectives. An audience of more than 200,000 people visited the exhibition, and it is estimated that over 2 million people were exposed to the exhibit in print and electronic media and that up to 250,000 were reached by the free distribution of the history booklet. In 1988 a smaller version of the exhibit was displayed through the sponsorship of

Figure 1.1. Latino Olympians Seminar, children and adults, 1984. *Photo by Antonio Ríos-Bustamante.*

the Eastman Kodak Company at the convention of the National Hispanic Chamber of Commerce in Washington, D.C. It is estimated that 20,000 people viewed it in the nation's capital (see Figure 1.2).

The Latino Olympian exhibit further demonstrated the potential of museum-quality Latino public history exhibitions in educating Latinos and the general public about important aspects of the 500-year history of Mexican Americans and Latinos. The success of the Latino Olympians exhibition and the "Two Hundred Years of Hispanic Theatre" exhibit also demonstrated the need for Latino history museums as well as the substantive inclusion of Mexican American history as part of the mission

A. Entrance to Latino Olympians Exhibit.

B. Visitors examine Latino history publications.

Figure 1.2. Latino Olympians Exhibit, Los Angeles, 1984.

of the large regional and national historical museums. A direct by-product of the Latino Olympians exhibition was the incorporation of the California Museum of Latino History in December 1984.

"The Life and Legacy of Dr. Ernesto Galarza"

Most Latino leaders and scholar experts on Latinos in the United States recognize the tremendous need to overcome long-standing myths and stereotypes about Mexican Americans and Latinos. An important aspect of overcoming stereotypes is through the correction of historical inaccuracies. Biographies of important Mexican American contributors to American culture play a major role in this process.

Because of the preponderant influence of anti-Latino stereotypes in U.S. popular thought, Mexican Americans are rarely considered to be people who exercise intellectual leadership. Yet there is a significant tradition of intellectual leadership in the Mexican American community.[21] The Mexican American and U.S. Latino communities produce women and men of high intellectual potential. Tragically, these abilities have been and continue to be ignored by society.

Nevertheless, outstanding Mexican American men and women have continued to excel. One of the most notable of them was a man born in great poverty who was to become an intellectual giant among the women and men of his generation. He was Ernesto Galarza, a Ph.D. in history and political science from Columbia University, an alumnus of Stanford University and Los Angeles Occidental College, founder of the National Council of La Raza, adviser to the Ford Foundation, and founder of the Mexican American Legal Defense and Educational Fund (MALDEF). Ernesto Galarza was also a "barrio boy" (the name became the title of a biography of his youth), a young Mexican immigrant who worked in the fields from childhood to support himself.

Galarza's life was an ideal theme for a biographical multimedia historical exhibit. It would demonstrate his numerous inspiring contributions as a scholar, educator, labor organizer, and elder statesmen in the Mexican civil rights movement and student movement.[22] During the centennial of Occidental College, the opportunity arose for officers of the California Museum of Latino History to produce an exhibition that would be part of a commemorative program about Galarza's life and legacy. The exhibit was the concept of William D. Estrada and Antonio Ríos-Bustamante, who became the producers, and was designed and constructed by Ernesto Collosi.

The Galarza family graciously consented to be interviewed for the exhibition and to lend numerous artifacts that had belonged to Dr. Galarza.

The exhibition was on display from April through May 1987 in the Occidental College library. A special feature of the opening was the dedication of a special Ernesto Galarza Room and the installation of a heroic bust of Galarza in the room. The exhibition depicted Galarza's life and legacy in a series of forty segments and included both mounted photographic enlargements and numerous items that had belonged to Galarza, such as his typewriter, eyeglasses, serape, and awards.

An estimated 10,000 visitors to the Occidental centennial viewed the exhibit, and another 200,000 people were exposed to it through media publicity. Several thousand more received copies of a commemorative program booklet that were distributed free of charge. The Galarza exhibition is an important example of a biographical multimedia exhibition featuring an outstanding Latino contributor to our society.

EXHIBITIONS AND PROGRAMS, 1980s–1990s
The San Diego-Tijuana Border History Fair

Another important and innovative type of applied history program is the history fair. An excellent example of this type of exhibition is the San Diego-Tijuana Border History Fair,[23] held annually from 1983 to 1990. It is important to emphasize that the San Diego-Tijuana Border History Fair was an international public history program. It is discussed here because it involved both Mexican Americans and Mexicans, as well as other groups.

The Tijuana fair provided an important example for other border communities and also a model for regional history fairs. It was initiated in 1983 as a binational program that would involve junior and senior high school students. Its goal was to promote awareness of the regional heritage and develop future leaders.

A binational coalition of organizations organized the fair, including the Universidad Autonoma de Baja California (UABC), San Diego State University, the San Diego Historical Society, and the San Diego and Tijuana schools. The fair was administered by the Institute for Regional Study of the Californias, San Diego State University, in cooperation with the Centro de Investigaciones Historicas de Tijuana.

The fair provided students from San Diego and Tijuana with the opportunity to develop historical projects, conduct research, build historical models and scenes, and present their findings in competition with other students at a three-day exhibition. The students at the first fair had the opportunity to develop original research projects derived from the overall theme of the "history of individuals, families, neighborhoods, events, institutions, businesses, and communities in the greater San

Diego-Tijuana region." Among the research projects were tabletop displays, audiovisual presentations, essays, and even dramatic and musical performances. Every year an overall theme was chosen for the fair, but projects could be done on any theme of the student's choice.

In 1990 the last fair exhibition was held on March 1–3 at the Universidad Autonoma de Baja California. The theme was "Ecological Changes and Technological Developments in the San Diego-Tijuana Region," with two age levels of competition: Junior, for students in grades 7–9, and Senior, for students in grades 10–12. There were seven categories of competition: (1) individual research paper, (2) individual exhibit, (3) group exhibit, (4) individual audiovisual presentation, (5) group audiovisual presentation, (6) individual historical performance, and (7) group historical performance. The organizers of the fair prepared a Spanish and an English "student guide," providing a description of the fair, the rules of competition, and a fair schedule.

The San Diego Tijuana Border History Fair is a truly outstanding model for the organization of international and regional history fairs. The fair was very successful, and annual attendance included the participation of over 7,000 students, 200 teachers, 150 community volunteers, and 11,000 visitors. Unfortunately, the fair lost its funding and was discontinued. Nevertheless, it remains an important model for Latino applied history programs.

"Where the Worlds Meet: The Mexican American Experience in Phoenix 1860–1987"

Organized by Phylis Cancilla Martinelli, Dr. Arturo Rosales, and Professor Cristine Marin, "Where the Worlds Meet" was a traveling exhibit of the history of the Phoenix Mexican American community, sponsored by the Arizona Council for the Humanities in 1987. The exhibit was supported by the Arizona Humanities Council and received assistance from J. C. Penney and the *Arizona Republic* and *Gazette*.[24]

National Reunion of Veterans of the Mexican Revolution, 1988

The National Reunion of Veterans of the Mexican Revolution is an outstanding example of an oral history project and commemorative program. The project began in 1973 when Dr. Manuel Urbina II, professor of Latin American history at the College of the Mainland in Texas City, Texas, began to collect information and conduct oral history interviews about the experiences of individuals alive during the Mexican Revolution.[25] Urbina states that the original idea for the oral history occurred to him when he was writing his doctoral dissertation about the Mexican side of the Texas revolution and could find no living persons to interview. He realized that there were still a significant number of veterans of the Mexican Revolution.

As his research and interviews continued, Urbina began to locate Mexican men and women who had not just experienced the revolutionary period but had been actual combatants in the various armies. His research was conducted not only in Texas but throughout the United States and in Mexico, where cooperation was established with the oral history program at the Universidad de Morelos in Cuernavaca.

The idea of a reunion occurred to Urbina when he organized a regional event in August 1987 that brought two veterans of the Mexican Revolution together in Houston. This meeting generated great public interest and attracted national press coverage. The strong positive public interest stimulated Urbina to develop the idea of a national reunion.

Urbina successfully sought support from the president of the College of the Mainland in Texas City (located in the greater Houston metropolitan area). As a result of his continuing research, by 1988 he had located and interviewed eleven Mexican veterans of the revolution who resided throughout the United States. Scattered from New York City to Los Angeles, these men and women ranged from eighty-eight to ninety-one years of age. Besides the veterans themselves, Urbina also established contact with the daughters of Generals Francisco Villa and Emiliano Zapata.

Planning for the National Reunion of Veterans of the Mexican Revolution involved contact with the Mexican Council General in Houston to secure the participation of a Mexican government representative in the event. The reunion was scheduled for November 20, 1988. Due to illness, only seven of the eleven veterans were able to plan to attend, and ultimately, only four veterans were actually able to attend. Tragically, one suffered a heart attack the night before the event.

Held in the college auditorium, the reunion consisted of a 6-hour program with official representatives present from Mexico and the state of Texas. A photographic display about the history of the revolution, which Urbina had created, was also on exhibit. The honorees included veterans who had fought in the armies of Francisco Villa, Emiliano Zapata, Venustiano Carranza, and Victoriano Huerta. Also present were Doña Alicia Villa, a daughter of General Francisco Villa, and her mother.

The program attracted 1,000 people, including 600 Mexican Americans, 350 Anglo-Americans, and 50 African Americans. Three hundred fifty of the attendees were students and 650 were community people. The reunion attracted outstanding media coverage. Major stories were carried in four local Houston daily newspapers and on four local television stations. At the national level, the story was carried by the AP, UPI, and Reuters and ran in the *Washington Post* and the *Wall Street Journal.* It was also carried by *Excelsior* in Mexico City and in the Mexican and Central American media.

"El Rancho in South Texas: Continuity and Change from 1750"

Curated by Joe S. Graham and exhibited at the John E. Conner Museum, Texas A&M University, Kingsville, "El Rancho in South Texas" depicted Mexican settlement and ranching in the *valle de Texas* from 1750 to the present. The exhibit involved eleven consultants, including David Montejano, Jose Roberto Juarez, Arnoldo De Leon, Andres Tijerina, and experts from the Smithsonian Institution.[26]

"The Chicano Experience in Arizona"

Curated by Christine Marin, curator of the Chicano Archives, Arizona State University, "The Chicano Experience in Arizona" opened at the Desert Caballeros Western Museum in Wickenburg, Arizona, on June 17 and ran through October 15, 1995. The exhibit illustrated the contributions of Chicanos in Arizona. It was derived in large part from the Alicia and Dora Quesada collection of photographs and manuscripts preserved at Arizona State University.[27]

Chicana Public History Programs

A particularly significant project has been developed by Dr. Denise Segura and other Latina scholars in the organization Mujeres Activas en Letras y Cambio Social. This group of Latina social scientists has assembled a slide show on the history of Mexican American and Latina women which has been shown in the northern California area and at past conferences of the National Association for Chicano Studies. The project is an important prototype that needs to be extensively duplicated. Numerous other Latino local slide and small-scale photographic exhibitions have been developed nationally and need to be systematically surveyed, with copies placed in a central archives.

Chicano Art History Archives

Significant efforts have been made in the fine arts to create an archive of Chicano/Latino art, including mural documentation at the Mural Resource and Education Center, Social and Public Art Resource Center (SPARC), in Venice, California. This collection includes slides of 30,000 murals from around the world.[28]

The California Ethnic and Multicultural Archives (CEMA), located at the library of the University of California, Santa Barbara, houses the archives of the Chicano Art, Resistance and Affirmation (CARA) exhibition.[29] CEMA also holds the papers of many Latino cultural and literary figures and organizations, including those of dramatist Luis Valdez and El Teatro Campesino theater company. A major component of CEMA is the Proyecto Caridad, which is involved in primary documentation of the works of leading Latino artists and arts institutions.

The Smithsonian Institution's Archives of American Art is strengthening its U.S. Latino holdings. It is acquiring primary source materials on Latino artists and photographers, including personal papers, and houses a collection of 3,505 slides documenting 741 Chicano murals in California.[30]

Family History and Genealogy

An especially significant area for Latino public history is family history and genealogy. Hispanic genealogy developed from the research of genealogists and historians in California, New Mexico, and Texas.[31] During the 1960s and 1970s, stimulated by state genealogical societies and media focus on Alex Haley's *Roots*, an increasing number of people were attracted to family history research.[32]

As a result, a number of regional Hispanic genealogical societies were organized that have a significant Mexican American involvement. Among them are the Society for Hispanic History and Ancestral Research in Fullerton, California; Los Californianos, the Hispanic Genealogical Society of Houston, Texas; Los Bexarenos of San Antonio, Texas; the Spanish American Genealogical Association of Corpus Christi, Texas; Los Porciones Genealogical Society in Edinburg, Texas; the Spanish American Museum, Albuquerque; the New Mexico Genealogical Society; the Genealogical Society of Hispanic America, Denver, Colorado; Los Descendientes in Tucson, Arizona; and Los Californianos, California. Several important genealogical journals are published by these organizations, including *SHHAR* (Society of Hispanic Historical and Ancestral Research) (see Figure 1.3), *Hispanic Genealogy*, and *Antepasados*.[33] These journals contain valuable historical information and analysis. Rare documents and lists of records are frequently reprinted with critical commentaries.

The existence of these organizations and their often extensive genealogical documentation programs reflects the tremendous potential interest in Latino family history and genealogy. Professional genealogists, some affiliated with the Utah Genealogical Society, have done much to stimulate this interest and even more to make available records of genealogical and historical value in documenting the Mexican American heri-

Figure 1.3. SHHAR (Society of Hispanic Historical and Ancestral Research) Family History Exhibit at Rancho Los Amigos, Downey, California.

tage. Among these genealogists are George Rykamp and Dr. Lyman Platt.[34]

The number of local and regional Hispanic genealogical societies is expanding rapidly, as are the quality and size of their programs. For example, in October 1995 the sixteenth Texas State Conference on Hispanic Genealogy and History was held in San Antonio.

There is a tremendous need for the establishment of regional and family history programs. University libraries, such as the University of California, Santa Barbara's Mexican American Studies Library, have made important contributions in creating archival repositories for late-nineteenth and early-twentieth-century Mexican American documents that have been largely ignored by publicly funded museums.

Regional and Community History

A program that has combined regional and family history is the Mexican American Regional and Family History program of the University of Arizona's Mexican American Studies and Research Center (MASRC), in Tucson. This program seeks to network with both scholarly and community groups to collect, preserve, and document the Mexican American heritage of Arizona. Important aspects of the MASRC Regional and Family History program are its Alianza Hispano Americana and Mexican American Mining Communities projects. These projects seek, respectively, to document the history of the largest Mexican American fraternal society of the early twentieth century and the important contributions of Mexicans to the mining industry.

In New Mexico the Southwest Hispanic Research Institute at the University of New Mexico developed the Barelas project, which seeks to systematically document Mexican American community history in the Albuquerque barrio of Barelas.[35] The Barelas project resulted in the development of a large-scale photographic exhibit that has toured New Mexico and was displayed at the 1991 Albuquerque conference of the National Association for Chicano Studies. The Oral History program of the University of New Mexico has begun "Impact Los Alamos: Traditional New Mexico in a High-Tech World, 1945–1995," which will examine the impact of the federal laboratories at Los Alamos on Native New Mexicans.[36]

In Riverside, California, the exhibit "Nuestros Antepasados (Our Ancestors): The Riverside Mexican American Community 1917–1950" was mounted at the Riverside Municipal Museum from May to November 1995. The exhibit, with Dr. H. Vincent Moses as curator, focused on the family histories of the Mexican settlers of Casa Blanca, East Riverside, and Agua Mansa.[37]

LATINO INITIATIVES AT THE NATIONAL LEVEL

A stronger Latino presence is needed at the national level, with new initiatives by national museums and by museum and historical associations. This must include long-and short-term plans for the recruitment, hiring, training, and promotion of Latino personnel, development of major permanent Latino history exhibits, appropriately funded programs, and the appointment of high-level Latino curatorial, program, and administrative personnel.

To date, however, the support of national museums and museum and historical associations for Latino public history programs has lagged behind that for Latino art, public art, and folkloric and artisan cultural programs.[38] This includes significant interest in Latino museums emphasizing fine arts.[39] Limited Latino programming by the Smithsonian museums on U.S. Latinos has emphasized the art, folk art, and photography of Latinos. No historical program or exhibit has yet been developed, with the partial exception of "El Rancho in South Texas: Continuity and Change from 1750" (discussed earlier), which was supported by the Smithsonian's National Museum of American History.[40]

A national initiative should include strengthening the efforts by the American Association of Museums and the Smithsonian Institution, and the start of new efforts by the American Association for State and Local History and the National Council on Public History. Major initiatives should be undertaken by the National Museum of American History and the National Museum of Natural History of the Smithsonian Institution.

Since 1992 a new effort to involve Hispanics in the Smithsonian Institution has occurred as the result of pressure by the National Council of La Raza and other groups. This effort is an outgrowth of the debate over the nature of commemorations of the Columbian quincentennial (1492–1992) for Native American/Latino history in the United States. During the quincentennial the Smithsonian created a program addressed to Latinos, who began to receive increased but still limited symbolic institutional attention.[41]

This attention was reflected in a minute increase in the hiring of Latinos to work in and coordinate some quincentennial programs such as the one at the Office of Public Programs of the National Museum of American History of the Smithsonian Institution in Washington, D.C. A modest series of official public historical programs about Latino heritage also received support.[42]

During 1992 token efforts were made at the National Museum of American History by hiring one or two highly qualified Latinos in the area of public programs. At this time Latinos in the Smithsonian's quincentennial program and other Latino museum professionals formed a Hispanic interest group within the American Association of Museums.[43] The Latino caucus has met annually at the meeting of the AAM.[44]

The Smithsonian has responded to pressure from these groups by forming a Hispanic Advisory Council[45] and by organizing the Latino Graduate Training Seminar in Qualitative Methodology with the Inter-

University Program for Latino Research.[46] A report on "Willful Neglect: The Smithsonian Institution and U.S. Latinos," conducted under the auspices of the Hispanic Advisory Council on the status of Latinos in the Smithsonian Institution, revealed a dismal picture.[47] The Smithsonian responded by creating and staffing the office of Counselor for Latino Affairs to "assist in the implementation of its Latino initiatives."[48]

It is imperative that the Smithsonian's Hispanic initiative continue and expand to other major museums. The expanded hiring of Latinas and Latinos needs to be at the curatorial level and in that portion of the executive staff charged with development and approval of program content. The Smithsonian and other major museums need to have executive staff members who are not merely aware of the existence of Latinos, Puerto Ricans, Mexican Americans, and Cubans and our history, but actually have professional knowledge of that history.

Unfortunately, most museums and public history programs either ignore, through ignorance, the contributions of Mexican Americans and other Latinos or distort our history through elitist interpretations that follow a historiography and ethnology forty years out of date. Such programs emphasize institutions, institutional elites, and European colonizers or native collaborators over the history of the majority of Mexicans. Museums and public history institutions that have not even begun to seriously incorporate Mexican Americans on their staffs beyond the level of groundskeepers or maids are neither aware of nor able to incorporate the last twenty years of historical and cultural research that Mexican American scholars have produced.

Regionally, an example has been set by the Gene Autry Western Heritage Museum in Los Angeles. Chicano historians had heavily criticized the Autry for ignoring or stereotyping Mexican American history.[49] The Autry eventually responded in a positive manner by changing the content of certain exhibits and by creating a permanent exhibit, "The Spirit of Community in the West," which provides an up-to-date interpretation of the cultural diversity in the West of the 1890s. This exhibit includes segments on Mexican, Chinese, Indian, African American, and European groups.[50]

LATINO PUBLIC HISTORY IN THE TWENTY-FIRST CENTURY

Those who support Mexican American history must, above all, recognize that Latino public history programs are produced and created by Latino professionals on Latino historical themes. Such programs incorporate the body of historical knowledge that has been accumulated in and by the Latino community. This information has been made available through the research of Mexican American and other Latino professionals.

It is now time for real change, for the recognition of Mexican American and Latino applied history programs as important and worthwhile in the field. Public historians and the executive officers of museum programs must recognize that their nap or siesta is over as far as Latino applied history is concerned.

ENDNOTES

1. Robert W. Righter, "Public History," *The Social Science Journal* 25, no. 4, 1988.
2. Edith Mayo, "Women's History and Public History: The Museum Connection," *The Public Historian* 5, no. 2 (1985). Raymond Starr, "The Role of the Local History Course in a Public History Curriculum," *The Public Historian* 6, no. 3 (1987).
3. Warren Leon and Roy Rosenzweig (eds.) *History Museums in the United States: A Critical Assessment* (Urbana: University of Illinois Press, 1989). Also see Louis R. Harlan, "The Future of the American Historical Association," *The American Historical Review* 95, no. 1 (February 1990), 3.
4. This was also the case with the Los Angeles County Museum of Art until recently.
5. Howard Morrison, *American Encounters* (Washington, DC: Smithsonian Institution, 1992). Other participants included co-curators were Richard P. Ahlborn, Richard P. Doty, and Rayna Green; Benito G. Cordova, researcher; and Harold Closter, project manager. Also see exhibition brochure, "American Encounters," National Museum of American History, 1991.
6. David Andrews (ed.), "Africa's Legacy in Mexico: Photographs by Tony Gleaton" (Washington, DC: Smithsonian Institution Traveling Exhibition Service, 1993). This has a bilingual text translated by Evelyn Figueroa.
7. Herman J. Viola and Carolyn Margolis, *Seeds of Change* (Washington DC: Smithsonian Institution Press, 1991). See also the exhibition brochure, "Seeds of Change: 500 Years of Encounter and Exchange," National Museum of Natural History, 1991. One of the few United States Latino participants was Joseph P. Sanchez, who contributed to the exhibition's commemorative book.
8. Samuel P. Nesmith, *The Mexican Texans* (Austin: Institute of Texan Cultures, 1981). Thomas Sheridan, *From Rancho to Barrio* (Tucson: Arizona Historical Society, 1985).
9. For example, a seminal debate in the development of Mexican American historiography concerns the issue of the continuity of the historical development of the Mexican people in the United States before and after 1900. Dr. Arthur Corwin, a Latin Americanist, argued that "Mexican American history" was invented by Cary McWilliams, author of *North from Mexico*. This

resulted in a critical response from leading Mexican American historian Dr. Rodolfo Acuña. See Arthur F. Corwin, "Mexican American History: An Assessment," *Pacific Historical Review* 42 (August 1973), and Rodolfo Acuña, "To the Editor," *Pacific Historical Review* 43 (February 1974).

10. For a discussion of Chicano filmmakers and films with historical significance, see Gary D. Keller (ed.), *Chicano Cinema: Research, Reviews, and Resources* (Tempe, AZ: Bilingual Press, 1984).

11. An example of an exceptional historical and cultural exhibition is the 1985 display of the Mexican theater exhibit, "El Pais de las Tandas," produced by the Museo de Culturas Populares in Mexico City. Depicting the Mexican *teatro de revista*, this exhibit is the counterpart of Nicolas Kanellos's "Two Centuries of Hispanic Theatre in the United States." The 1985 exhibition was also exceptional in that a significant effort was made to show the very real linkages of the *teatro de revista* in Mexico and in the Mexican and Spanish-speaking communities of the United States. Dr. Carlos Vasquez, who coordinated the presentation of "El Pais de las Tandas" in Los Angeles, was instrumental in establishing the Mexican/Mexican American linkages.

12. Shifra M. Goldman and Tomas Ybarra-Frausto, *Arte Chicano: A Comprehensive Annotated Bibliography of Chicano Art, 1965–1981* (Berkeley: Chicano Studies Library Publications, University of California, 1985).

13. The transfer of the former El Pueblo de Los Angeles State Historical Park to the city of Los Angeles was engineered by Los Angeles Councilman Richard Alatorre. The transfer itself and the continuing process for development at the park have sparked controversy between Mexican American merchants on Olvera Street (organized in the Olvera Street Merchants Association), various groups that are concerned with the type of preservation and historical themes at the park, and potential concessionaires aligned with Councilman Alatorre, who seek to develop various segments of the former state historic park. Mexican American historian Rodolfo Acuña has written periodically in the former *Herald Examiner* and more recently in the *Los Angeles Times* regarding the concern that the park is being gutted to enrich developers and that the Mexican heritage theme there is threatened. See Rodolfo Acuña, "In '88 Latinos Must be Vigilant, and Not Forget," *Los Angeles Herald Examiner,* January 1, 1988, A15.

14. See the introduction to *Five Views* (Sacramento: California Department of Parks and Recreation, 1988).

15. Jose Pitti, Carlos Cortes, and Antonia Castañeda, "A History of Mexican Americans in California," in ibid.

16. Antonia Castañeda, "Sites," in ibid.

17. See Antonio Ríos-Bustamante, "What the California Museum of Latino History Can Do and Why," *La Red/The Net* 1, no. 2; Rodolfo Acuña, "Power Grabbers Threaten Dream of Latino Museum," *Los Angeles Herald Examiner,* January 28, 1988, A15; Antonio Ríos-Bustamante, "California Museum of Latino History: Feasibility Report," Prepared for the State of California, Los Angeles, April 1986; Ford Foundation, "Black and Hispanic Museums," New

York, 1990. The effort to develop Mexican American public history programs has also included the Organization of Latino Museums. Several of the Latino museums now being created include plans to develop both cultural and historical programs. These include the Mexican Museum in San Francisco and the newly organized Museo Chicano in Phoenix. The Mexican Museum has existed for over a decade and has developed exhibits of Mexican folk art. The Museo Chicano was developed by Chicanos Por La Causa, a community development organization, and is housed in a new 10,000-square-foot facility at the El Mercado Mall in Phoenix. The California Museum of Latino History has been producing exhibits since 1984. It has led the effort to create a state-supported museum program comparable to the 60,000-square-foot Afro-American Museum at Exhibition Park in Los Angeles.

18. Virginia Escalante, "Photo Exhibit of L.A.'s Latino Legacy," *Los Angeles Times*, September 16, 1981. Also see Antonio Ríos-Bustamante, "The Photo History of the Mexican Community of Los Angeles, 1781–1981," *Caminos*, September 1981, and "The Once and Future Majority," *California History* LX, no. 1, April 1981.

19. Nicolas Kanellos, "Two Centuries of Hispanic Theatre in the Southwest," *Revista Chicano-Requena* XI, no. 1 (1983). Nicolas Kanellos (ed.), *Hispanic Theatre in the United States* (Houston: Arte Publico Press, 1984). Nicolas Kanellos, *Mexican American Theatre: Legacy and Reality* (Latin American Literary Review Press, 1987).

20. Gary Liebman, "Exhibits to Spotlight Minorities' Olympic Role," *Los Angeles Times*, December 29, 1983. Virginia Escalante, "Exhibit to Commemorate Contributions of Latino Athletes on U.S. Olympic Teams," *Los Angeles Times*, June 6, 1984. Antonio Ríos-Bustamante and William D. Estrada, *The Latino Olympians: A History of Latin American Participation in the Olympic Games, 1896–1984* (Los Angeles: Sponsored by the Los Angeles Olympic Organizing Comittee, 1984). Antonio Ríos-Bustamante and William D. Estrada, *The Latino Olympians: A Pictorial History, 1896–1990* (Encino, CA: Floricanto Press, forthcoming).

21. For a discussion of this tradition see Mario Garcia. *Mexican Americans: Leadership, Ideology, and Identity, 1930–1960* (New Haven, CT: Yale University Press, 1989).

22. William D. Estrada and Antonio Ríos-Bustamante, "The Life and Legacy of Dr. Ernesto Galarza: 1905–1984" (Los Angeles: California Museum of Latino History, 1987).

23. Information was provided by Dr. Paul Ganster, Director, Institute for Regional Study of the Californias. See Institute for Regional Study of the Californias, *San Diego-Tijuana International History Fair: Student Guide* and *Instructivo para Participantes* (San Diego State University, 1990). Mark Arner, "San Diego, Tijuana Students Gain Cultural Knowledge in History Fair," *San Diego Tribune*, March 3, 1988, B7. Anthony Millican, "Students Breathe Life into History in Campus S. D.-Tijuana Exhibit," *San Diego Union*, March 4, 1988, B1. Fernando Romero, "Student Projects Build Border Ties," *San Diego Trib-*

une, March 5, 1989, B1. Barbara Valois, "Students Discover a Fair Exchange," *Los Angeles Times,* February 25, 1988, San Diego County Section, 1.

24. "Where the Worlds Meet: The Mexican American Experience in Phoenix 1860–1987," brochure.

25. Information for the National Reunion of Veterans of the Mexican Revolution was provided by Dr. Manuel Urbina III. See Program for the National Reunion of Veterans of the Mexican Revolution, November 20, 1988. Elizabeth Hudson, "A Few Who Were There Recall Mexico's Revolution," *The Washington Post,* November 21, 1988. Jan Ried, "Compadres de la Revolucion: Five Veterans of Mexico's Bloody Struggle Recall Riding Through the Whirlwind of History with Villa and Zapata," *Texas Monthly,* November 1988, 122.

26. Joe Stanley Graham, *El Rancho in South Texas: Continuity and Change from 1750* (Denton: University of North Texas Press, 1994).

27. Brochure, "The Chicano Experience in Arizona" (Tempe: Chicano Archives, Arizona State University).

28. SPARC statement, "Social and Public Art Resource Center," p. 1. The Mural Resource Center (MRC) is said to have the most extensive collection regarding twentieth-century muralism in the United States. SPARC was founded by Chicana muralist Judith F. Baca, painter Christina Schlesinger, and film maker Donna Deitch in 1976.

29. Proyecto Caridad, *Chicano Art: A Resource Guide* (CEMA, University of California, Santa Barbara, September 1991); Connie V. Dowell, "Rare Resources: Ethnic Archives Help Balance Scholarly Perspectives," *Coastlines,* Winter 1992; Connie V. Dowell, "Collecting Primary Materials of Major Ethnic Groups," *College Research Libraries News,* March 1992. CEMA, "Multicultural Archives Home Page."

30. "Archives of American Art Seeks Latino Materials," *La Smithsonian* 1, no. 2 Fall/Winter 1995.

31. Contributors prior to the 1960s included Marie Murillo Northrop, Frey Angelico Chavez, Carlos Castañeda, Works Progress Administration writers, and the Utah Genealogical Society.

32. This included such well-known researchers as Rudecinda LoBuglio, George Ryskamp, Lyman Platt, historian Bill M. Mason, and many others.

33. The *SHHAR* is published by the Society of Hispanic Historical and Ancestral Research, Fullerton, California. *Hispanic Genealogical Journal* is published by the Hispanic Genealogical Society of Houston, and *Antepasados* is published by Los Californianos. The Society of Hispanic Historical and Ancestral Research also publishes a membership bulletin, *Somos Primos.*

34. George Ryskamp is a faculty member of the department of history at Brigham Young University. Lyman Platt is the director of Instituto de Genealogico e Historico Latinoamericano, St. George, Utah.

35. Brochure, "Barelas Project," Southwest Hispanic Research Institute, University of New Mexico.

36. Brochure, "Impact Los Alamos: Traditional New Mexico in a High-Tech

World, 1945–1995," The Oral History Program, University of New Mexico, Albuquerque, 1996.

37. Dr. Bruce Harley, "Hispanics Featured Riverside Museum," *Somos Primos,* Autumn 1995, 22.

38. An excellent summary of Chicano exhibitions is Jacinto Quirarte, "Exhibitions of Chicano Art: 1965 to the Present," in Richard Griswold del Castillo et al. (eds.), *CARA: Chicano Art: Resistance and Affirmation* (Los Angeles: Wight Art Gallery, University of California, 1991). The developing interest in Latino art and art programs is reflected in new literature on multicultural programs. Museum literature on multiculturalism includes Bernard Young (ed.), *Art, Culture and Ethnicity* (Reston, VA: National Art Education Association, 1990) (this includes no contribution specifically on Latinos and none by Latino authors); Russell Ferguson et al. (eds.), *Out There: Marginalization and Contemporary Cultures* (Boston: The New Museum of Contemporary Art and MIT Press, 1990) (includes contributions by Gloria Anzaldúa, "How to Tame a Wild Tongue," pp. 203–211, and Richard Rodriguez, "Complexion," pp. 265–278); and Ivan Karp et al. (eds.) *Museums and Communities: The Politics of Public Culture* (Washington, DC: Smithsonian Institution Press, 1992 (includes Guillermo Gomez-Peña, "The Other Vanguard," pp. 65–75, and Alicia M. Gonzales, "Companeros and Partners: The CARA Project," pp. 262–284). One of the few essays actually discussing a Latino historical cultural exhibit is Michael Heisley, "Collections and Community in the Generation of a Permanent Exhibition: The Hispanic Heritage Wing of the Museum of International Folk Art," in Kenneth L. Ames et al. (ed.), *Ideas and Images: Developing Interpretive History Exhibits* (Nashville: American Association for State and Local History, 1992. This discusses the "Familia y Fe" 1990 exhibit at the Museum of International Folk Art, Santa Fe, New Mexico.

39. Barbara Y. Newsom and Adele Z. Silver, "Community Based Museums and Umbrella Agencies," in Newsom and Silver, *The Art Museum as Educator* (Berkeley: University of California, 1978). Descriptions of the major Latino art museums, including San Francisco's Mexican Museum; Chicago's Mexican Fine Arts Center Museum; New York's El Museo del Barrio; and Denver's Museo de Las Americas are given in Patti Sowalsky and Judith Swirky, *On Exhibit: The Art Lover's Travel Guide to American Museums* (New York: Distributed Art Publishers, 1995).

40. See op. cit., note 27.

41. The Smithsonian Institution's Quincentenary program was headed by folklorist Dr. Alicia Gonzales.

42. These programs included exhibitions on the encuentro and on New Mexico.

43. Smithsonian Institution Latino Working Committee, "The Latino Caucus, Networking for the Future," American Association of Museums, 88th Annual Meeting, Fort Worth, Texas, 1994.

44. The AAM Latino interests network began publishing a newsletter, *L.I.N. News,* in 1994.

45. Members of the advisory council include Tomas Frausto Ybarra, chair; and Raul Yzaguirre, executive director of the National Council of La Raza.

46. Announcement, "The Inter-University Program in Latino Research and the Smithsonian Institution present the 1994 Latino Graduate Training Seminar in Qualitative Methodology, Interpreting Latino Cultures: Research and Museums," 1-page broadside. The Latino Graduate Training Seminar in Qualitative Methodology was coordinated by Dr. Gilberto Cardenas and is modeled on the experience of the Latino Graduate Training Seminar in Qualitative Methodology, since 1987 run jointly with the Social Science Research Council. A similar program, a summer seminar, was first proposed by the IUP's Latinos in Museums Working Group in 1992 as part of the Latinos in Museums, Public History, and Art Project proposal. Letter, October 9, 1992, Maria Chacon, associate director, Inter-University Program for Latino Research regarding proposal and suggesting Latino museum research agenda meeting. The Latinos in Museums Working Group held a Latino Museum Research Agenda planning at the Mexican Museum in San Francisco in 1992. The agenda resulting from this meeting was used in planning the present anthology, *Latinos in Museums: A Heritage Reclaimed.* Participants in the agenda meeting included Christine Marin, Arizona State University; Antonio Ríos-Bustamante, University of Arizona; Maria Chacon, IUP; Tomas Ybarra Frausto, Rockefeller Foundation; Veronica Gonzales, University of Texas; Marie Acosta Colon, Mexican Museum; Cynthia Orozco, University of Texas; Sylvia Orozco, Mexic-Arte, Austin; Carlos Tortolero, Mexican Fine Arts Center Museum, Chicago; Juana Guzman, National Association of Latino Arts and Culture, Chicago; and Karen Boccalero, East Los Angeles Self-Help Graphics.

47. Smithsonian Institution Task Force on Latino Issues, *Willful Neglect: The Smithsonian Institution and U.S. Latinos* (Washington, DC: The Smithsonian Institution, 1994).

48. *La Smithsonian: A Smithsonian Institution Latino Affairs Newsletter* 1, no. 1, Summer 1995. The office is headed by Dr. Miguel A. Bretos, counselor for Latino Affairs.

49. Rodolfo Acuña, *Los Angeles Herald Examiner.* Acuña and other scoholars criticized the Autry Western Heritage Museum for a theme mural with an Old West theme depicting Mexicans as bandits and prostitutes. The only other theme at that time representing Latinos emphasized the conquistadors Coronado and De Soto.

50. Gene Autry Western Heritage Museum, "The Spirit of Community in the West." Other exhibits that have reflected Mexican American history include an interactive exhibit based on the history of the Ruelas ranch, located near Tucson, Arizona, and a program on the "Zorro" film character curated by John Langellier.

2 DIVERSITY WITHIN DIVERSITY: LATINOS OF SOUTH FLORIDA

Martha Gutierrez-Steinkamp

The American Association of Museum's Annual Conference in Seattle, Washington, in 1994 provided a unique opportunity for participants to hear Martha Gutierrez-Steinkamp and her fellow museum professionals, Jose Aguayo and Dolores Calaf, address the topic of cultural and regional diversities and obstacles facing Latino groups in the United States. In their straightforward presentations to the conference participants, Gutierrez-Steinkamp, Aguayo, and Calaf took to task, and rightly so, those museum directors, program coordinators, curators, and museum historians who have failed to consider Latinos and Latinas for professional positions within their museums, centers, or historical society settings. The speakers' analyses of the complexities of being Latino and facing obstacles such as racism, discrimination, and ignorance from the dominant society are vitally important to the future direction and administration of cultural institutions and museums. Gutierrez-Steinkamp's chapter reflects the concerns of her colleagues in the context of the cultural issues facing Latinos in South Florida and the rest of the nation.

—The editors

FACT: By the year 2010 "Hispanics" will become the nation's largest "minority"—22 percent of the total population of the United States (U.S. Census 1990).

THE QUESTION OF LANGUAGE

Once I suggested that a certain museum provide labels in English and Spanish as an incentive to attract tourists. I was asked, would these labels in Spanish be understood only by Cubans, since I am from Cuba. I suppose they thought I speak "Cubanese Spanish." Latinos speak Spanish (except Brazilians, who speak Portuguese, and people who speak French in the smaller Caribbean islands). The Spanish language is the thread that binds us. While a word may be used in a different context in a particular country, that does not mean there are many kinds of Spanish, just as there are not many kinds of English. In Great Britain people speak of the "lift," while we call it "elevator" in the United States.

FACT: Spanish was the first European language spoken in the present-day United States. Spanish speakers represent 54 percent of all non-English speakers in the United States. Spanish missions mark the first non-Indian presence in Arizona and California.

THE QUESTION OF DIVERSITY

The Spanish who arrived following Columbus's voyages were a culturally diverse people. The Iberian Peninsula received political, economic, and cultural influences from several powerful Mediterranean civilizations: Phoenicians, Greeks, Celts, Iberians, Visigoths, Romans, and ultimately the Moors. After their expulsion from Spain, the country was unified beginning with the reign of Isabella and Ferdinand in the fifteenth century. Shortly after, the Spanish explorers arrived in the Americas.

The people who awaited them in these lands were culturally diverse as well. In the Caribbean the Arawaks and Tainos were very different from the Caribes, and these groups were very different from the Olmecs, the Mayas, and the Aztecs, who in turn were very different from the Incas. The Andean civilizations from the mountain ranges of South America lived in virtual isolation and developed their own language, religion, and culture. With the arrival of the Spanish, among some peoples there was almost total acculturation; among others there was not.

Racially, the Spanish are *not* different from other Europeans. People from northern Spain are like other northern Europeans—with fair skin and blue or green eyes. Those from the south or Mediterranean, like other southern Europeans, are olive-skinned and have dark hair. The Irish, Germans, and Italians who immigrated to the United States were not referred to as minorities or grouped into an Irish/Italian/German race. While some discrimination did exist, particularly in the case of Catholics, these people were not considered to be of a different race, nor was a name invented to classify them as a group by the government or anyone else.

As for the native peoples of the Western Hemisphere, those in the United States are called Native Americans, and all others referred to as Indians. Yet the first of them to come in contact with the European explorers were those in the Caribbean and Mexico, who were Native Americans too. In most instances they lived in far more advanced social and political structures than those living in what today is known as the United States. Evidence of this can be seen at such historic sites as Chichén Itzá, Tulum, Palenque, and Machu Picchu, to name a few.

"And Now We Are Discovering Diversity?"

Beginning with Fort Mose in Florida over 250 years ago, there have been culturally and racially diverse populations living in the same area in the United States. African slaves escaping from English-owned plantations in the Carolinas found freedom with the Spanish in St. Augustine.

In 1783, when more than one hundred runaway slaves arrived in St. Augustine, the Spanish governor of Florida established the fort and community of Fuerte Gracia Real de Santa Teresa de Mose. The former slaves were granted their freedom and moved into the fort, becoming part of the Spanish militia. They made important contributions to Florida's multiethnic heritage.

In the late nineteenth and early twentieth centuries, Cuban exiles trying to regain their country's freedom from Spain settled in many parts of the United States, including New York and Key West.

FACT: Between 1870 and 1920, immigration from Europe was so high that about one of every seven residents of the United States was born in another country, the highest foreign-born percentage of the total population in history (U.S. Census 1990).

FACT: In 1907 immigrants added 3 percent to the U.S. labor force. That is the equivalent of 9 million immigrants joining the U.S. workforce in one year today (U.S. Census 1990).

THE LATEST INFLUX AND NEW CULTURES

Recent immigrants have come from different parts of the Americas. In what may be the most diverse immigration, many of the arrivals have been political refugees.

A significant change in Florida's population began in the early 1960s after Fidel Castro took over the Cuban government. In the late seventies and the eighties, political exiles from Central and South America joined the Cubans and moved into banking and international trade. By 1990 more than a half million Cubans had settled in Dade County. Latinos from the Caribbean and Central and South America accounted for 10 percent of Broward County's population and 7 percent of Palm Beach County's.

Many Latino immigrants are not fluent in English, but this does not make them illiterate. English-speaking people moving to France who speak little French are not considered illiterate, retarded, or backward.

Nevertheless, communication is the "game of the future." Those of us who can communicate in more than one language will be ahead in the game—just as people who have computer skills will be. Bilingual individuals are not a threat to their fellow workers but rather a source of additional knowledge.

High expectations were placed by teachers and families on those of us who grew up in bilingual (Spanish-English) surroundings. We were required to perform at our best in both languages. There was never an assumption that we were "handicapped" or "learning disabled" or any other label used in societies for learners of a second language. More important, there was no need to sacrifice one's native language for the other.

FACT: Between 1980 and 1990, immigration reached its second-highest level ever. The latest wave of immigrants came from the Caribbean and Asia (U.S. Census 1990).

FACT: A common definition of *Hispanic* is someone with a Spanish surname.

THE "LABELING" SYNDROME: DEFINITION OF LATINO IDENTITY

People often ask what is the difference between Hispanic, Latino, and Chicano. "Which is the correct one to use"?

The term *Hispanic* is used by the government to identify those of us who come from Latin America. The term is used erroneously to indicate that we are of a different race.

Social and political activists prefer *Chicano*, which emphasizes their Indian heritage and speaks out against what is perceived as the repressive and genocidal conquest of the indigenous people of the Americas by the Spaniards. Others prefer Mexicano, Guatemalteco, Hondureño, Panameño, Chileño, Peruano, and so on, retaining loyalty to their former homeland.

As for the term *Latino*, there is no single Latino community. The name Latin America stems from the fact that the languages spoken in the area all derived from Latin.

There are many diverse Latino communities in cities throughout the nation. In the Southwest and Texas, towns across the border from Mexico have overwhelming Mexican populations. In New Mexico, where the

Spaniards settled twenty-two years before the Pilgrims landed at Plymouth Rock, the Spanish-speaking population is still slightly larger than the non-Spanish-speaking. The southern half of the state of Colorado has a significant concentration of Latinos, and many place names there are Spanish. In the Northeast, the diverse Latino population, of which Puerto Ricans are the largest group, are likely to be younger and geographically concentrated in urban settings, with the highest concentration of Latinos in Massachusetts.

The colonial relationship between Puerto Rico and the United States began in 1902 following the Spanish-American War. It was characterized by massive North American capital investment in the industrialization of Puerto Rico. Since the Jones Act of 1917, Puerto Ricans are by birth U.S. citizens.

The first Puerto Rican families relocated to New York back in the 1930s and from there extended their family networks throughout New England. Puerto Ricans are the only Latinos who migrate to the mainland in circular migration patterns, due to their U.S. citizenship status.

Some people in the United States disagree with the concept of neo-tribalism. It goes against the idea of "American" unity expressed by our national slogan, E Pluribus Unum—One Out of Many. We should all call ourselves Americans. However, there is a problem with this concept.

When Columbus landed in the so-called New World, he arrived at a small island in the Atlantic Ocean and from there proceeded to Cuba, Puerto Rico, and other islands. Subsequent explorations by Columbus and those who followed him produced settlements in Mexico, Central and South America, and the areas known today as Florida, Louisiana, Texas, New Mexico, Arizona, and California. Thus it would seem that those of us who are Spanish-speaking are the only ones who can truly be called Americans, not those who are descendants of the Pilgrims and other groups who arrived in the new lands more than one hundred years after the Spanish.

FACT: No anthropological system of racial classification uses the term "Hispanic" as a term of racial identification.

RACIAL DIVERSITY, CULTURAL DIVERSITY, AND CULTURAL INSTITUTIONS

In this "decade of diversity" most people don't know the difference between cultural diversity and racial diversity—including our cultural institutions, their staffs and boards, and our government. Latinos are racially diverse: white, black, yellow, red, brown. We are also culturally diverse; our ancestry can be European, American Indian, African, Asian, or all of the above.

We are not people of color if this refers to black and brown only. We are people of color if white and yellow are included, because we are white (those of us of European ancestry only) and we are yellow (those of Asian/Pacific ancestry). Latinos do not belong to a "Hispanic race." When an institution employs a Black/African American, unless this person was born in Latin America and speaks Spanish or Portuguese, it has not employed a Latino or anyone closely related to us.

The employment of Latinos in the cultural environment is in need of much improvement. In 1994 I conducted a mini-survey in fifty-two southeastern museums selected at random, asking three questions: (1) Do you employ Latinos? (2) In what capacity do you employ Latinos? (3) Would you be interested in information regarding the Latino Interests Network of the American Association of Museums?

Of the fifty-two museums surveyed, ten responded and only four employed Latinos. Two museums employed Latinos in assistant curatorial positions. One employed six Latinos in facilities maintenance. Another museum responded they had only four employees (does this preclude having a Latino as one of the four? I ask). Two museum directors indicated interest in receiving information regarding the Latino Interests Network.

I have lived in Florida for thirty years and know of only one Latino executive director of a Florida museum—me. I don't know of one institution where a Latino is employed as a community relations/liaison person or in any executive/managerial position. Latinos are invited to serve on museum committees in the effort to reach "minorities" in the community, but this kind of participation is not perceived by us as an invitation to a full partnership.

LATINOS IN MUSEUMS:
THE PRESENT, THE FUTURE

The Museum of Arts and Sciences in Daytona Beach has one of the finest collections of Cuban and colonial art. Most museum people in Florida don't know this and are not interested, either.

During the quincentennial celebrations in Broward County, we begged various local institutions to bring pieces of this collection to South Florida. The director of the art museum never returned our calls, and a board member informed us this collection did not fit their interests. The historical museum reluctantly agreed to host an exhibition of the Daytona collection but placed it in a back room where no one would find it.

It is precisely the lack of sincere interest and almost condescending attitude that keeps Latinos away from museums. It is also the fact that "interpretation" is often a source of irritation, resulting in alienation rather than inclusion.

In South Florida, arts councils are among the worst offenders. The American Association of Museums' document on "Excellence and Equity" is a step in the right direction, although the AAM's staff, boards, and committee chairs are virtually "Latino-free."

The Smithsonian has sponsored "the birth" of the Latino Interests Network and its activities through the Office of Education and Public Service, and is providing other opportunities through the Office of Museum Programs. However, the report *Willful Neglect*, issued by the Smithsonian Institution Task Force on Latino Issues, clearly presents a picture of an institution that is not representative of and responsive to the entire population of the United States.

The Southeastern Museum Conference (SEMC) has created a diversity committee, of which I am a member. There is a sincere desire on the part of this group to address important issues affecting Latino professionals and the audiences that SEMC institutions must serve.

If we are to embrace the ideas of excellence and equity for museums in the twenty-first century, our first commitment should be to show sensitivity to the changing demographics of our audiences. If we expect to communicate in a meaningful way with a growing Latino population, we need to see and understand the Latino community from their perspective.

The following strategies are examples of the steps that need to be taken toward the integration of Latinos in the museum world:

- Museums must recruit and train Latinos to work as members of interpretive teams in exhibitions and programs to gain the benefit of first-person experience.
- Museums must become aware of who are their community leaders and what are their resources. They must listen and assess Latino interests.
- Mentorship programs are greatly needed to train museum professionals and Latinos currently working in museums. Curators and others should use this opportunity to mentor those who will in time replace them.
- Established museums need to create equal partnerships with Latino community organizations and cultural institutions.
- On the other hand, Latino professionals need to become active members of museums as advisory board members, collections and program advisers, and trustees.

The process of joining, planning, brainstorming, participating in programs, and debriefing are steps for building community trust and ownership, thus resulting in more consistent and lasting participation as audiences, potential members and staff in museum settings.

The influx of diverse Latin American groups in the last twenty years, especially into the Southeast, presents an opportunity for cooperation, mentoring, and enrichment for all. Understanding our diversity within the population of our region, and given the opportunity, we will make major contributions both as Latinos and as citizens of the United States while preserving the cultural diversity of each group.

A partnership among all groups will ultimately enrich and empower all of us equally in this generous nation.

ONE LAST STATISTIC

The Florida Commission on "Hispanic" Affairs reports, based on the 1990 Census, has found that the state will achieve a ratio of representation, of community to government, within twenty-four years! Unfortunately, a statistic such as this is the norm throughout the country, not the exception. The challenge—both to our fellow Latinos and to our other colleagues—is to take the leadership as educators and representatives of cultural institutions and prove such statistics wrong.

3 EXHIBITING MESTIZAJE: THE POETICS AND EXPERIENCE OF THE MEXICAN FINE ARTS CENTER MUSEUM

Karen Mary Davalos

In this case study Karen Mary Davalos examines the problematics of the decontextualization of Latino art and artifacts in Mexican exhibitions in American museums; museum exhibition and collection policies; and the interpretation and representation of Mexican exhibits at the Mexican Fine Arts Center Museum in Chicago. The chapter examines five exhibitions held at the museum that exemplified, yet reconfigured, the Western museum tradition of objectifying non-Western cultural forms. Among the topics Davalos covers are the reterritorialization and recontextualization of space; the inscription of objects as aesthetic achievements; the problems of how and where objects are displayed; how objects are interpreted in labels and panels; and how the marketplace and museums have influenced the production of artisan craft objects in Mexico. The chapter concludes with consideration of the experience of Mexicano museum-goers, who bring their own perception of history to interpret and experience objects on display.

—The editors

Increasingly since the 1870s, the public museum in the United States has offered visitors a European-centered version of what is referred to as an "American" cultural heritage, a patriotic and sanitized interpretation of the nation's past, and an authoritative account of taste.[1] In the public history museum, commitments to founding fathers, heroes of war, and men of capital create an institution that resembles a shrine to patriarchy and capitalism, excluding the role of internal conflict, inequality, and women in the nation. The large urban art museums in the United States, such as the Metropolitan Museum of Art in New York and the National Museum of American Art in Washington, D.C., claim a commitment to

Western civilization, but they equate the West with Greece, Rome, Egypt, or Europe. Even the frenzy to remodel the public art museum so that it includes a new gallery or wing for non-Western art does not challenge the European-centered collection policy or, more important, the message that the entire citizenry traces its heritage to Europe. More revealing, the new galleries and wings do not shake off the evolutionary model of the public museum, in that they refer to non-European art as primitive, traditional, folk, or exotic.[2]

In fact, what is refered to as a public museum is the institution that presently condenses and categorizes history and experience. It is no longer the case that the side show, the circus, and the curio shop enjoy the same authority of the public museum as authors of the nation and educators of the citizenship.[3] According to Neil Harris, American museums in the first half of the nineteenth century were repositories of eclectic collections. Paintings and sculpture stood alongside mummies, mastodon bones and stuffed animals.[4] By the close of the nineteenth century, however, such curio collections as that displayed by Charles Willson Peale had lost their museum status and become instead a side show.

Like these collections, however, public museums continue to display a variety of objects, but they do so in a way that promotes a unifying message. All objects and peoples are appropriated into a genre of similarity through stories of shared origins and futures. When the public museum admits to difference, it is as if inequalities and conflicts between cultures do not exist, and the visitor is encouraged to view the world as if it "were a vast [landscape] of self-sufficient economies, each one in its own display case, unruffled by the proximity of others."[5] Public museums also classify such potentially troubling objects as foreign and exotic—outside the boundaries of the imagined nation.

Taken together, the narrative and the collections of the public museum make it unusually clear that ethnic minorities, women, homosexuals, the homeless, and other "deviants"—or from my perspective, we—are not part of the citizenship and the nation. The public museum does not collect our histories and experiences, particularly not our art. It does not categorize our cultural products as "American" but marginalizes them, even placing them in the hallways and other makeshift galleries. Native American art is surely the exception, as it has been the core of many collections since and even prior to the Museum Age (1870–1930)—though it has been warehoused or displayed in natural history museums as if it and its producers were akin to plants and animals,[6] not humanity, and certainly not the nation's masculine and patriarchal citizenry.[7] By ignoring history or by dehumanizing Native Americans, the public museum glosses over the truth of the United States, much of which has depended upon our ability to survive social injustice. Thus, as long as the public museum functions as a nation-building institution, it is necessary for us to create our own institutions.

In the 1970s and 1980s, African Americans, Mexican Americans, Puerto Ricans, Asian Americans, and Native Americans began to create their own institutions to represent, interpret, collect, exhibit, or promote the art and culture of their own communities.[8] Many of these institutions were established within the communities and neighborhoods. However, they were more than sites of cultural exhibition and production, as their artistic goals were inseparable from the social, educational, and political goals. At times they functioned as advocates for ethnic communities, often becoming directly involved in community development, political action, and protest.

It is not surprising, therefore, that the discourse surrounding these museums is often celebratory, narrating a heroic act of resistance and affirmation and opposing the public museum. Calling for a new history of the United States, these museums spoke of the experiences of people of color and social injustices such as slavery and genocide. In particular they challenged the public museum's representation of people of color, immigrants, women, and other "deviants" as noncitizens. For some artists and activists, it became necessary to reject, even demonize, the public museum, arguing that those who exhibited in the public museum were sell-outs to their own communities.[9]

Within the Mexican American community, the subject of this essay, Chicano/a scholars and artists have been reluctant to engage questions about how we exhibit or represent ourselves. During the height of the Chicano art movement, it was enough for many artists, activists, and scholars to produce relevant messages for their local communities and to work for change through art and exhibition. At the time it was assumed that self-representation and empowerment avoided the problems of collection and interpretation. Oppositional art was, after all, a contestation of the oppressiveness of capitalism, nationalism, imperialism, or other social injustices. Initially, however, not all social injustices were valid or authentic for oppositional artists; concerns of women, homosexuals, and biracial people were often excluded. Opposition was constructed as a pure and mutually exclusive condition which assumed the centrality of a masculine and heterosexual experience and celebrated cultures and peoples the public museum and the nation did not. It was unexamined how we could make the mistakes of the public museum, how the promotion of difference could also diminish heterogeneity, how an exhibition devoted to images of social injustice could gloss over inequality, and how self-determination could also recirculate the stereotypes about Chicanos and Mexicanos. In short, how could a counter-hegemonic institution practice nationalism?

MUSEUMS AS POLITICAL SITES

The first premise is that public museums are political sites which disclose how communities are constructed and how nations are imagined. As a site engaged in the politics of representation, it is not enough to describe the "beautiful" objects of a museum nor is it sufficient to announce the success of an exhibition. Cultural critics must examine the complex, multiple, and ambiguous messages signified by Chicano and Mexicano museums. I recommend that awareness in addition to promoting pride, self-determination, and positive cultural identity, the visual narrative in Chicano and Mexicano museums can also recirculate stereotypes about Mexicans.

The description of complexity and multiplicity is not intended to diminish the emotional significance and importance of Mexican museums and exhibitions for Mexicano visitors. It is not my goal to write as if I have discovered a terrible secret of Mexican art/culture exhibition. Rather, I want to explore the ambiguities of representational practices, especially within museums not initially designed for the nation. Therefore, as I examine Mexicano exhibitions, I tread carefully so that as problems and contradictions are uncovered, they do not appear as predictions for behavior or essential experiences of museum-goers. By paying attention to ambiguity, I attempt to bring to light the processes and forces at work in representation and, as Martín-Barbero advocated, to avoid applying binary theoretical models that obscure the complexities of mestizo experience.[10]

In fact, it is to *mestizo* experience, to life on the borders, that I want to look for a new way of thinking about cultures and the sites that organize and interpret cultures: in this case, the museum. Mestizo experience denies the rigid boundaries between cultures and nations usually proposed by public museums or nationalism. Mestizo cultures are more fluid, porous, and flexible than objectivism, popular belief, and dominant ideologies would have us believe. Mestizo experience cannot be considered from one perspective because it always originates from at least two places. In displaying mestizo experience, contradiction appears most clearly because we are so well versed in nation and nationalism. I suggest that we cannot confine Mexicano and Chicano exhibition to one geopolitical or cultural place—this side or *al otro lado*, "us" or "them." *Mestizaje* is both an expression of cultural affirmation and self-determination and a result of domination. It is the combination of these expressions that gives rise to the hybrid forms that are not "co-opted" or "authentic."

Ironically, the original discourse and promotion of mestizaje did not include hybrid experiences beyond the cultural. *Criollos* in New Spain limited their efforts to the recognition and authentication of the mixed heritage that had "created the unique Mexican people."[11] Their understanding of cultural hybridity (at the time called "racial mixing") excluded gender and sexuality. In fact, in revolutionary Mexico mestizaje was a strategy for nation building, and it "became the ideological symbol of the new regime."[12] I employ Gloria Anzaldúa's notion of mestizaje, however, which invokes hybrid cultures, genders, sexualities, languages, and voices. Located on the border, Anzaldúa's vision of mestizo experience works against nations, fixed identities, and harmony. Focusing on chaos, ambivalence, and the tension produced by culture contact, Anzaldúa insists on recognition of "this place of contradictions"[13] and find a "way of balancing, of mitigating duality"[14] by opening up to the queer, the "other," the female, and the indigenous.

Marcos Sanchez-Tranquilino and John Tagg put forward that the *pachuco* and *pachuca*, Mexican American urban youth of the 1940s, embodied mestizo hybridity.[15] They argue that the aesthetic style of the pachuco and pachuca—particularly their zoot suits (with wide shoulders and pleated, ballooning pants narrowing at the ankle), their beehive hairstyles, their *caló* language, and their defiant stance—broke boundaries. By dressing, speaking, and walking in ways that did not signify "America" or "Mexico," the pachuco and pachuca expressed "the dualities of rural and urban, Eastside and Westside [of Los Angeles], Mexican and American, and, arguably, feminine and masculine." These dualities were "not pure negation. Not *mestizo*—half and half—but an even greater *mestizaje*. A new space: a new field of identity."[16]

It is precisely this "new field of identity" that causes me to question the distinctions James Clifford made in his travel account of four Northwest Coast museums. Clifford suggested that public museums are distinct from community (or in his words, "tribal") museums, arguing that even though all museums are local, majority or public museums are designed to reflect a universal human heritage. Community museums, he contends, express the concerns of a specific population in opposition to the majority:

> (1) [The tribal museum's] stance is to some degree oppositional, with exhibits reflecting excluded experiences, colonial pasts, and current struggles; (2) the art/culture distinction is often irrelevant, or positively subverted; (3) the notion of a unified or linear History (whether of the nation, of humanity, or of art) is challenged by local, community histories; and (4) the collections do not aspire to be included in the patrimony (of the nation, of great art, etc.) but to be inscribed within different traditions and practices, free of national, cosmopolitan patrimonies.[17]

Although his attention to the art/culture subversion is useful, I indicate that the distinction between the "tribal" and the public museum allows us to imagine that these institutions are mutually exclusive. In this chapter I examine the visual narrative of a Mexicano museum, proposing that exhibition styles and interpretive techniques can work within nationalism or recirculate the ideological location of the Mexican immigrant within United States nationalism. More important, the visual narrative of a Mexicano museum might reflect both opposition and accommodation because it borrows display techniques from the art museum and the ethnography museum. In general, my argument differs from Clifford's in that I do not view opposition as a discrete and fixed entity but something that is slippery and porous. I prefer to describe the exhibition of Mexicano art and culture as mestizaje, a hybrid form whose very existence interrogates the binary objectivism that has imagined people and cultures as discrete, seamless wholes.

In addressing mestizaje, this chapter has two goals. The first is concerned with the visual narrative of a Mexicano museum. I examine the complexity, multiplicity, irony, ambiguity, and accommodation expressed in the representation of Mexicano art/culture at the Mexican Fine Arts Center Museum (MFACM).[18] I suggest that although this Mexicano museum is bounded somewhat by the conventions of display and histories of imperialist collecting, it simultaneously works against the powerful conventions of representation to create a hybrid form. The second goal is concerned with the experience of Mexicano museum-goers. What happens when Mexicanos enter an exhibition? The visual narrative of the museum, borne of resistance and accommodation, does not signify one meaning but multiple meanings as each visitor passes through the museum using his or her own history to interpret and experience the objects on display.

Mexican Fine Arts Center Museum: "For Our People" and "For Everyone"

Founded by two educators, Carlos Tortolero and Helen Valdez, the Mexican Fine Arts Center Museum (MFACM) opened its doors on March 27, 1987, in Chicago's Pilsen neighborhood, a predominantly Mexicano community since the mid-1960s.[19] As an institution, however, the MFACM has coordinated and produced exhibitions since its incorporation in 1982. During its first five years, the museum sponsored over twenty-four events and programs, including a folkloric dance concert and exhibition seasons in 1983, 1984, and 1985.[20] The Mexican Fine Arts Center Museum is the first Mexican museum in the Midwest and as of 1996 had produced over thirty-five exhibitions, with shows touring the

United States and Mexico. The exhibition season is divided into four areas: the annual exhibition for El Día de los Muertos (the Day of the Dead), contemporary art, traditional art, and Mesoamerican art/artifacts. In addition to the visual arts, the MFACM is also dedicated to the performing arts, music, and dance. Performing artists have included Nobel laureate Octavio Paz, actress Ofelia Medina, critic and writer Carlos Fuentes, and MacArthur fellows Guillermo Gómez-Peña and Sandra Cisneros, as well as the specifically Chicano rock group, Dr. Loco's Rockin' Jalapeño Band.

The MFACM is a nationally recognized museum, particularly because of its outreach and education programs. In 1992 it was selected to participate in the Marshall Field's Chicago Arts Partnerships in Education, a program designed to enhance arts curriculum within the public school system and to create art-centered schools. Working in partnership with local elementary schools in the Pilsen/Little Village area, the MFACM has advocated for and helped establish Orozco Arts Academy, an elementary school devoted to fine arts curriculum. In 1995 the MFACM was identified as a recipient of the National Museum Services Award (see Figure 3.1). Also in that year, the MFACM received a $475,000 grant from the Pew Charitable Trust to plan and launch "*Puentes*: Bridging Cultural Communities," a four-year project to build cross-cultural understanding through collaborations with art institutions in Chicago and Mexico.

Finally, the Center Museum's notion of "promoting Mexican culture" includes advocacy and action for the Mexicano community. The MFACM collaborates with community-based organizations to increase the number of day care centers, to enhance arts curriculum, and to improve education, housing, and the political power of Mexicanos. The museum also functions as a liaison for artists to local arts councils, arts institutions, and publicly funded arts programs.

The MFACM emerged at the moment when Latinos found an opening in Chicago's remaking of itself. Former Mayor Harold Washington, the first African American mayor in the city of Chicago, built a coalition among people traditionally ignored by Chicago's Democratic machine. This coalition, or at the least the discussion of such unity, opened a discourse never before imagined at the political level. Historically Chicago had been conceived of as a black-and-white city, and city politics were established along these lines, which excluded something not black or white. The coalition allowed Mexicanos and other Latinos to expand the black/white discourse. The MFACM is one of several community-based cultural centers and organizations to emerge from the political shift that established Mexicanos as players in the metropolitan arena. During the 1970s and early 1980s, Mexicano leadership demanded and won local and federal funds to support social service centers, drug rehabilitation

Figure 3.1. Museum Services Award to Mexican Fine Arts Center Museum (MFACM) by Hillary Rodham Clinton. Left to right: Carlos Tortolero, executive director; Sylvia Ortiz-Revollo, chair, MFACM. *Photo courtesy the White House.*

centers, cultural institutions, and education programs. The Center Museum continues to play an active role in city programs that affect Mexicanos, particularly those in the Pilsen and Little Village neighborhoods.

In fact, the mission statement of the MFACM constructs the institution as a site between cultural groups; that is, mestizaje is the Center Museum's design. Although the primary goal of the museum "has been to conserve and preserve for our people,"[21] both Tortolero and Valdez state that the primary goal supports a secondary goal of outreach to non-Mexicanos. Valdez contends that outreach allows the MFACM to "confirm our reality as a community."[22] The mission statement illustrates how the MFACM imagines itself in the city, the region, and the nation(s):

> The Mexican Fine Arts Center Museum evolved out of a commitment to awaken the City of Chicago to the wealth and breath of the Mexican culture, as well as to stimulate and preserve the appreciation of the arts of Mexico in the city's large Mexican community.
>
> The Mexican Fine Arts Center Museum is the first Mexican cultural center/museum in the Midwest and the largest in the nation. The Museum has the following goals: to sponsor special events and exhibits that exem-

plify the rich variety in visual and performing arts found in the Mexican culture; to develop and preserve a significant permanent collection of Mexican art; to encourage the professional development of local Mexican artists; and to offer arts education programs.

The Mexican Fine Arts Center Museum serves as a cultural focus for the more than half a million Mexicans residing in the Chicago area and it also serves as a cultural ally to other Latino cultural groups in the City of Chicago.

As a site for cross-cultural contact, the MFACM is constructed on a metaphorical border between Mexico and the United States. This border exists without nationalist and geopolitical claims. The events sponsored by the MFACM do not come from Mexico or the United States but from "the Mexican culture," which can exist "anywhere Mexicans have gone."[22] In addition, the border is a site where conflict is resolved. During an interview with management analysts Michele Nadanyi and Mark Parry Tortolero explained it this way:

> The museum is for every Mexican in the world, our honor is at stake; we want both the local community and the mainstream world to visit . . . so that we can break down some of the barriers. . . . If only our own people come here, we will have failed in our mission. We really believe that this is a place for everyone.[23]

Though not imagined as one, the Mexican Fine Arts Center Museum is a public museum, "a place for everyone." Similar to the other eight museums on city park property, such as the Adler Planetarium, the Art Institute, the Chicago Historical Society, the DuSable Museum, the Field Museum of Natural History, and the Shedd Aquarium, the Center Museum is a member of the Museums in the Park and receives a proportion of the parks tax levy.[24] In 1994 the MFACM received approximately 38 percent of all its operating funds from the tax levy. In that year members of the Museums in the Park committed to a ten-year capital bonds budget for the MFACM. In addition, it applies for and receives grants from public bodies such as the Illinois Arts Council, the Chicago Department of Cultural Affairs, and the National Endowment for the Arts. Third, admission to the Center Museum is free, which grants visitors not only access but a sense of ownership. It is a museum for the public.

Art and Ethnography Museums: Inscribing Objects and People

In order to understand how the MFACM mixes display techniques and aesthetic styles and thus complicates representation, how art museums and ethnography museums treat objects, how they inscribe objects, and how the message is conveyed through the style of display must be examined.[25] Thus, my focus on the public museum concerns how it produces particular ideas and beliefs and is itself a "product of social and political interests."[26]

Art museums arrange objects individually or in isolation from one another. This display style is generated from the premise that the objects on exhibition represent a unique example of a style or school, the achievement of an individual, or the authoritative example of taste or beauty. Upon viewing an original artistic statement, the student of art feels a thrill of emotion and a heightened sense of being.[27] The "untutored visitor" can understand or appreciate the object if the visitor is permitted to glimpse beauty or fine taste unencumbered by didactic labels and display elements.[28] "Focusing on a single object facilitates the concentration necessary for the aesthetic experience to occur."[29] In fact, nothing—including the color of the walls, the lighting, the identifying labels, the hardware, the security rope, and other architectural elements—should distract the viewer from seeing and experiencing each object one at a time.

In the art museum an object's social location and historical context are erased; the object has no additional meanings, messages, or background outside its aesthetic qualities. As Douglas Crimp pointed out, the object in the art museum refers "only to itself—'itself' indicating both its material essence and the self-enclosed history of the medium."[30] Therefore the assertion that objects "belong to no particular place" allows curators to pretend that objects simply materialize at the museum's doorstep.[31] It is not necessary to discuss their acquisition, the terms of their collection, or their route from personal object to art market.

Removed from their original historical context, art objects implicate a larger, universal history, suggesting that all visitors (at least those visitors who resemble the image of the nation: men, heterosexuals, and Anglo-Saxons) share origins and experiences with "beauty." The premise of universality is even more apparent in the ethnography museum, which is based on a modern impulse to construct a "continuous evolution from ancient times" to the present.[32] The invention of universal origins conceals conflict, difference, and incompatibility and by default implies that the objects on display represent the heritage of all current populations. Beyond universalism, however, ethnography museums have little else in common with the art museum.

The significant difference between the art museum and the ethnography museum is that ethnographic exhibitions are driven by interpretive ideas, not form. Objects are employed to convey a particular concept, place, or relationship so that they signify products (or artifacts) of a culture, not the inspiration of specific individuals. Constructed as artifacts and not fine art, objects are displayed along with didactic labels, charts, time lines, tables, or diagrams and *with other* objects. In fact, early ethnographic exhibits were distinguished by their clutter and density of objects. Although labels provide historical and social information, they rarely acknowledge the individual or individuals who created the object, since objects are intended as the achievement of a cultural group. This approach suggests that individuals who create objects are not as important as the curators, anthropologists, or adventurers who "recover" the object or the person who purchases the object. The anonymity of the producers makes it difficult for audiences to visualize living people or to mistake the objects as the essence of the culture group. Both interpretations suggest that the population on display is dead, quantifiable, monographic, and faceless.[33]

This interpretation is closely associated with the ethnography museum's imperialist and nationalist origins. The ethnography museum (and the proto-art museum) was initially designed to display the trophies of imperial conquest, an intention that has translated into a classificatory scheme for civilizations as primitive or advanced, traditional or modern, and savage or human. Sally Price argues that the ethnography museum's concern with classification (primitive, stone age, developing, industrial) serves as an organizing strategy to produce cultural differences and distance, imagining entire populations as "us" or "them."[34]

MEXICANO EXHIBITION:
NEW MESSAGES AND MEANINGS

Exhibitions sponsored and organized by the Mexican Fine Arts Center Museum employ a range of display techniques and interpretive strategies.[35] For example, as in the art museum, objects are frequently isolated on podiums and behind Plexiglas. Displayed like original treasures, objects are set in isolation from one another using light, space, and color. Works are assigned a brief label identifying the artist, the name and date of the work, the medium, and the name of the person or institution who loaned the work. Exhibitions that tour the United States and Mexico locate objects within an international fine arts aesthetic and market. For example, the traveling exhibition "Art of the Other Mexico: Sources and Meanings" (June 18-September 12, 1993)—the first international touring exhibit of Mexicano and Chicano artists that was organized and curated by Mexicanos and Chicanos—inscribed the objects as aesthetic achievements and gained recognition from the international fine arts community. In fact, all objects exhibited at the MFACM—from the paintings created by local schoolchildren, the *retablos* of the nineteenth and twentieth centuries, the sculpture of Juan Soriano, the photographs of Agustin Victor Casasola to the mural-like paintings of Alejandro Romero—are presented as fine art, an attribute invoked in the museum's name.

Similar to the ethnography museum, the MFACM uses techniques to establish the object's social context. Using highly visible and linguistically accessible didactic labels written in both Spanish and English, the MFACM provides information such as the artist's life history and motivation for creating the object, the symbolism within the object, the intentions of the artist, or the events and feelings portrayed by the object. At the entrance to many exhibits, lengthy explanatory labels provide the visitor with a larger social history of the objects on display. This type of historical information is intended to make objects relevant to visitors, to present information omitted by local school curricula, and to promote a sense of ownership by connecting objects to sociopolitical issues and community concerns. The strategy to connect current political events with the content of the work locates objects in the realm of self and nation, private memory and public action.

At first glance it is ironic that the MFACM borrows aesthetic styles and display techniques from the art museum and the ethnography museum. Not only do these museums have contrary approaches to objects and people, but the Center Museum's concern with self-determination and affirmation are compromised by these approaches. For example, the interpretive strategy of isolating objects and presenting them as individual artistic achievements is curious in a museum that emphasizes community, not individualism. And the strategy of inscribing objects as artifacts —the debris of "dead" cultures—is problematic in a museum that encourages its visitors to view Mexicanos as living constituents in the city of Chicago. Similarly, the display of objects as if they were aesthetic achievements undercuts the premise on which Mexicano and Chicano art is based—that it exists in a particular cultural, political, and social context.[36] Can a Mexicano museum reclaim objects by simply displaying them in a finely appointed gallery? Finally, the interpretive strategy and display techniques of the ethnography museum suggest that peoples and cultures are coherent, bounded, and timeless. By suggesting a monographic or monolithic Mexican culture, does the MFACM undermine its central premise of diversity and complexity?

This study argues that the mixing of aesthetic styles and display techniques produces unanticipated results that rupture the message initially conveyed in the ethnographic or artistic approach to objects. In what follows, I examine select exhibitions at the MFACM: "The Amate Tradition"; "Popular Toys of Mexico"; "Mexico, La Vision del Cosmos"; and "The Day of the Dead." For each exhibition, I discuss how it ruptures the original visual narrative of public museum by reconfiguring the art/culture distinction, by deterritorializing the nations of Mexico and the United States, and by locating objects in histories of domination and dispersal. In addition, I examine how exhibitions are complex sites of cultural representation that produce a variety of messages and experiences, some of which work in tension with messages of affirmation, liberation, and resistance.

Art/Artifact/Souvenir

The Center Museum's exhibit of "The Amate Tradition: Innovation and Dissent in Mexican Art" (January 27-May 28, 1995) raised questions about the art/artifact distinction and explodes the two categories by elevating a third category: souvenir. This exhibit showcased contemporary *amate* (bark paper) paintings created by Nahua artists from the Alto Balsas region in the state of Guerrero. Amate painting emerged in the mid-1960s as potters, influenced by commercial markets, changed their medium from ceramics to bark paper. The exhibit recognized that amates are souvenirs, or tourist art, but repositions them as historically and politically situated objects of fine art. As narrative paintings, amates include a range of expressions: private nightmares, personal dramas, reinterpretations of European icons, pastoral utopias, social commentary, and public protest.[37] Dissenting voices were the center of the exhibition, particularly those that illustrate the "struggle against the planned construction of a hydroelectric dam that would have forced the relocation of forty thousand people" living near San Juan Tetelcingo.[38] Reinterpreting a religious figure, amate artists transform Saint James (Santiago), whose presence in Mexico can be traced to the Spanish conquest, into a "dauntless defender of indigenous rights."[39] Through Santiago, the amate paintings narrate two futures: one in which the dam destroys the inhabitants of the Balsas River basin and another in which the builders of the dam are swept away in an attack led by Santiago. By allowing these objects to retain their political content and by locating them in a specific historical moment, the exhibition played with and challenged the categories of fine art, "tradition," and tourist art.

In addition, the amate paintings were displayed with a retrospective exhibit of Balsas Region ancient and contemporary ceramics and wooden objects, the precursors of amate painting, in order to demonstrate the transition of images from three-dimensional to two-dimensional surfaces. This part of the exhibit traced the production of Balsas Region ceramics from ancient civilization to contemporary practice among families. Focusing on the recent production of ceramics for market, thus for aesthetic rather than utilitarian purposes, the exhibit explored how ceramics became a commodity on the international market beginning in the 1930s as the government, Mexican intellectuals, and commercial and private buyers increased, stimulated, and circulated their production. More important, the exhibition recognized the role of individual expression, family contributions, and government agencies such as FONART (Fondo Nacional por las Artesanías) in the production and circulation of both amate paintings and pottery, thus not allowing the museum visitor to imagine a timeless and pristine "traditional" or masculine culture. Together, the amates and the pottery signify cultural innovation and self-determination among indigenous men and women.

Interestingly, the exhibit had more to offer. Thirty photographs accompany the amate paintings. The Introductory Panel at the MFACM refers to the photographs as "ethnographic"; that is, they are positioned as records of the daily life and environment of the Nahuas, not as the creative work of José Angel Rodriguez, the principal photographer. The introductory panel continues: the photographic "exhibit [is intended] to foster a more profound appreciation for the creative spirit, political awareness and individual identities of Nahua artists who paint on amate."[40] Therefore, unlike conventional ethnographic displays of indigenous people that encourage an evolutionary perspective and anonymity, the photographs affirm the creative, politicized identities of specific Nahua artists. At the same time the photographs are a backdrop for the amate exhibit, referencing the aesthetic achievement and the political and social contexts from which the objects originate. Together, the exhibition contests the public museum's anonymous approach to so-called tourist art, folk art, and indigenous people.

The amate exhibit illustrates that Mexicano exhibition operates on multiple and often conflicting levels. First, the exhibit is a display of art and artifacts. However, it also interrogates the art/culture distinction and suggests an alternative hybrid location for the amate as souvenirs of resistance. Second, the exhibit challenges the assumption that so-called tourist or folk art is apolitical. What remains unanswered is how amate paintings circulate in the cultural memory of Chicago's Mexicanos. Does the Mexicano museum visitor share in the reclaiming of amate paintings as fine art, since for her or him Mexico is not a vacation place but a homeland?

Deterritorializing and Recirculating Nations

The exhibition "El Juguete Popular Mexicano/Popular Toys of Mexico" (March 1-June 9, 1991) signifies multiple and potentially ambivalent narratives: affirmation/liberation and accommodation/domination. "El Juguete" showcased over one thousand toys of Mexico from the collections of the Museo National de Artes e Industrias Populares and Casa de las Artesanías del Estado de Michoac n. Similar to the amate exhibition, "El Juguete" reinscribed popular art as fine art.

> The toys of Mexico have a distinctive aura of folk fantasy about them. They are also among the most abundant and imaginative in the world. Fashioned from a vast range of materials, they reveal, possibly more than any other craft, the ingenuity and inventiveness of their creators. Yet, because of the ephemeral nature and low commercial value of these objects, toy makers are rarely recognized for their skills. Toys are frequently overlooked for serious study and [we believe] the need to establish a museum exclusively for toys, in Mexico, is apparent.[41]

Text from the exhibit reveals how the MFACM repositioned and affirmed personal and everyday items as objects for serious art collection. However, unlike the amate exhibit, "El Juguete" suggests that emotions are central to exhibition programs, not just artistic ability and skill: toys have a "special place in the hearts of people of all ages."[42]

It is unclear, however, if the exhibition signals a transnational community—Mexicanos and their toys throughout North America—or Mexican nationalism.[43] Hand-crafted toys, along with particular festivals (i.e., El Día de los Muertos), cultural groups (Oaxaceños), and pre-Columbian civilizations (Aztecs), have been promoted by the Mexican government since the Porfiriato in an effort to homogenize an otherwise diverse citizenry.[44] From the start, Mexican nationalism was conceived as necessarily homogeneous, and political and social leaders have tried to diminish or erase Mexico's indigenous diversity. Jesús Martín-Barbero points out how the homogenizing effects of nationalism have resulted in the circulation, collection, and marketability of select popular arts, including toy making, at the expense of other cultural practices. More critically, García Canclini argues that Mexican government agencies sanction particular festivals, objects, and peoples in order to develop capital and the tourist economy.

Given this history, an exhibition of toys is not simply a celebration of the "ingenuity and inventiveness" of artists but a confirmation of the nation: in this case, Mexico. The recirculation of Mexican nationalism is problematic for a cultural institution that challenges national boundaries and questions national authority.[45] Thus, while the exhibit affirms the everyday items and emotions of Mexicanos and thereby recognizes and authorizes toy makers as creators of fine art and as national cultural treasures, the exhibit awkwardly supports a nationalism that denies the existence and identity of the Center Museum's founders and members.

Ambiguity, Chaos, and Creativity

"Mexico, La Vision del Cosmos: Three Thousand Years of Creativity" (January 31–May 31, 1992) featured over 150 objects on loan from the Field Museum of Natural History, representing over 3,000 years of Meso-american or pre-conquest civilization. Not only does the exhibition invoke a history of conflict and inequality, but the objects resonate with the tension between Western imperialism and objectifying social science.

The exhibition was part of a season of programming dedicated to a revisionist history of the encounter between the Americas and Europe. The text of the introductory panel and exhibition catalog explains the Center Museum's intentions for the exhibition.

> Nineteen ninety-two is a milestone year for people of the Americas. It marks the 500th anniversary of an invasion, not a discovery of the Americas. The fact that many people want to see this event as a discovery and want to celebrate it as such is ludicrous if anyone analyzes the consequences of this encounter. To call it a discovery is to deny both the millions of people who are already living in the Americans and their cultural achievements. The reality, and it is not a pretty one, is that millions of Native Americans of North America, Central America, South America, and the Caribbean were killed or died from the various diseases that were brought from Europe. Hundreds of indigenous cultures were destroyed in the process. Millions of Africans were inhumanely brought over as slaves, with hundreds of thousands dying in a process that endured for over three hundred years. It was both a human and cultural genocide.[46]

One hundred fifty-eight objects are positioned as a recognition of the conflict produced by the cross-cultural contact between the Americas and Europe. In addition, the objects call attention to an unequal relationship and the persistence of indigenous cultures. Moreover, the exhibition suggests that people who celebrate "discovery" are implicated in the "human and cultural genocide" produced by this cultural encounter.

Beyond the interpretive move to relocate objects as a sign of resistance, the design of the exhibition invokes mestizo experience. Thus, pre-Columbian objects address at least two perspectives. First, the objects are described as fine art, as creative achievements. However, they are more than aesthetic accomplishments, as they affirm the taste, skill, and development of Mesoamerican civilizations, demanding equal authority with

European fine arts. Second, they are displayed in an ethnographic style
with a time line, maps, dioramic murals, and detailed explanatory labels.
Operating as artifacts, the objects represent that ancient presence in
Mexico, a history that does not depend upon validation from Europe but
demands its own criteria.

The MFACM's unique accomplishment of producing this exhibition,
however, is complicated by the fact that the exhibition depended on the
Field Museum of Natural History's Starr Collection. The objects on display—a small part of the Starr Collection—are a contemporary result of
the very encounter to which the Center Museum refers in the introductory panel. During the last decade of the 1800s, Dr. W. D. Powell, the first
Southern Baptist missionary to Mexico, excavated and eventually sold
the objects on display to Frederick Starr of the University of Chicago.
Described as a "business associate" of anthropologist Starr, Powell excavated the objects from ancient graves, an inhumane practice currently
challenged by indigenous populations.[47] The objects signify the Spanish
conquest and the Field Museum's part in United States imperialism. The
objects are artifacts of these unequal encounters.

At the same time the objects—usually in storage at the Field Museum
of Natural History—remind us of a past when "the material properties
of tribal peoples were classed with strange flora and fauna, as objects of
wonder and delight, to be collected as trophies, souvenirs, or amusing
curiosities during one's travels to far and distant lands."[48] The objects
have not moved out of a natural history museum and into an art museum,
specifically Chicago's Art Institute, because they retain their exotic properties. In fact, catalog essayist Donald McVicker refers to the shaft tomb
effigy figures as "prize items in any collection of Prehispanic art."[49] Finally, the Field Museum's requirement of a security guard raises other
complications for the Center Museum. From whom does the guard pro-
tect these objects? Who can claim ownership of these objects? Descendants of Mesoamerican civilizations, anthropologists, or grave robbers of
Mesoamerican civilizations?

Mestizaje, however, denies coherence and completeness. The mestizo
space created through the exhibition of Mexicano art and culture is an
ambiguous location made of chaos and creativity. That is, Mexicanos create new coordinates when they exhibit themselves and refer to their own
cultural products as artifacts, focusing on survival and innovation, not
bygone days and peoples. "Mexico, La Vision del Cosmos" is "quite possibly the first time that an exhibit of pre-Columbian artifacts, many of
which have never been shown before, has ever been exhibited within a
Mexican community in this country."[50] The exhibition is perhaps one of
the best examples of "first voice" representation, a practice that recog-

nizes the conventional approach to the interpretation of objects but encourages new meanings, actors, voices, and sources.[51] From the "first voice" perspective, Mexicano exhibits do not necessarily move objects into distant coordinates but closer to Mexicanos. That is, the presentation of objects works not to produce difference between groups but to establish familiar cultural property.

Exhibiting Mestizaje: Día de los Muertos Practices

A discussion of mestizo experience would not be complete without an examination of Día de los Muertos practices. The Day of the Dead is itself a cultural product that resulted from cross-cultural encounters. It signifies a contact zone between Spanish Catholicism and pre-Columbian cosmologies, and it has more recently been reinvented in the United States as Mexicanos and Chicanos reclaim their cultural heritage. Chicago's first public practice of the Day of the Dead was organized by Clay Morrison in 1981 at the West Hubbard Gallery. The Mexican Fine Arts Center Museum officially recontextualized the practice in 1987 with the opening of their annual Día de los Muertos celebration (see Figure 3.2).

By moving the practice into the Center Museum, the cultural products of and for the Day of the Dead shift in meanings. In the home and at the cemetery, altars and altar makers, usually women, are connected through intimate and personal experiences. The altar is a private space of worship, homage, and faith created out of intimate knowledge and experience with the deceased. In the MFACM the secular combines with the sacred as well as the market. (The Center Museum's store sells *calaveras* and other objects traditionally associated with *ofrendas*.) At the same time the everyday practice of altar making is sanctified as fine art, now referred to as "installations." That is, they provoke both an aesthetic response and a religious experience.

The ofrendas/installations at the MFACM are commemorative, collective, individual, private, and public. Each year several artists, youth groups from schools, and local practitioners create ofrendas/installations that pay homage to family and friends. These personalized works share space with ofrendas/installations that communicate a political message, an innovative practice that challenges concepts of authenticity and tradition. For example, in 1988 Laura Gonz lez created an ofrenda/installation for the victims of the September 1985 earthquake in Mexico City. In that same exhibition Carlos Cortez created an ofrenda/installation dedicated to the people around the world and throughout history who died because of racial, religious, or cultural intolerance and oppression. Cortez commemorates the Aztecs of Tlatelolco, the Jewish uprising in Warsaw, and the massacre at Wounded Knee. In 1990 Mario E. Castillo

A. Altar honoring Cesar Chavez

B. Neighborhood drinking buddies from the Chicago 18th Street
neighborhood.

Figure 3.2. Día de los Muertos, Mexican Fine Arts Center Museum, Chicago.
Photos by Antonio Ríos-Bustamante.

created an ofrenda/installation for Vincent Van Gogh on the one hundredth anniversary of his death.

In 1992 the MFACM reconstructed the Day of the Dead and the annual exhibition as part of the season's revisionist project, providing another "Meaning of Día de los Muertos: 500 Years of Resistance" and making it a marker for cultural survival, inequality, and oppression. Crossing back and forth between political (public) and intimate (private) issues, the exhibition did not refer to religious practices or traditional celebrations as apolitical events. Instead, like "Mexico: La Vision del Cosmos," the 1992 Day of the Dead exhibit challenged the "discovery" myth of the Americas and celebrated the ability of indigenous peoples to resist devastation.

> During the last 500 years, many of these indigenous groups have continued to resist their eradication. Mexico in particular is fortunate to still have the contributions of 56 different indigenous groups who have struggled to maintain their rich cultures, languages, and traditions. One of the most beautiful and moving of the traditions which has endured over the centuries is the *Día de los Muertos*. Although contemporary manifestations of this tradition incorporate Catholic elements, it is essentially an indigenous tradition.[52]

The Day of the Dead is repositioned as resistance to the conquest, unmasking the discourse of discovery as another imperialist move. The exhibit also suggests that the Day of the Dead is more than an echo of the past; it is a symbol of a possible future of cultural and human survival. Of course, this exhibit is not without its complexity and ambiguity. The use of strategic essentialism nearly freezes in time "indigenous tradition" while it allows the Center Museum to reclaim an indigenous authenticity and authority in the contemporary practices of Día de los Muertos. That is, claims to an essence may bind and fix indigenous culture, but it also establishes the discourse for indigenous survival and resistance.

MEXICANO MUSEUM VISITORS AS ACTIVE SUBJECTS

Mexicano exhibition techniques are powerfully reinscribed by Mexicano visitors who rework, and at times displace, the dominant narrative of the public museum and the nation regarding immigrants. Moving objects into unanticipated spaces and meanings, Mexicano museum-goers dislodge the curator's concerns with fine art or artifact as they employ their own senses and claim the objects for themselves.[53] I suggest that Mexicanos perform the "ritual of citizenship" at the Mexican Fine Arts

Center Museum[54] but that this ritual creates a new nation and museum as well as an identity that does not depend on nationhood.

Most Mexicanos learn at a young age that public museums are not made for them but instead are institutions closed off to them. In addition to the cost of museum membership or entrance tickets, the security guards and ropes convey that we don't belong. More important, the language, message, and focus of the public museum excludes us. At the Center Museum, however, Mexicanos are the experts, intimately familiar with the images, icons, and messages of the objects on display. Their cultural literacy is particularly powerful because the MFACM speaks to them as the site of authority and in the first person: these objects are ours. This authority and sense of entitlement or ownership is a unique experience for Mexicanos, as most public museums erase them. Finally, Mexicanos find within these exhibitions a homespace, a territory of belonging, as they are transformed into owners and creators of a culture.[55] Their citizenship, imagined by the practice of Mexicano exhibition, rewrites the dominant narrative about the American citizen, since it invokes multiple cultures and histories *sin fronteras* (without borders). However, because this homespace is lacking territory, the Mexicano body itself becomes the location for nation, community, and culture.

What are the implications of the new citizen and new nation? What types of actions do mestizo representational practices invoke? I suggest that Mexicanos—moving between their homespace and the geopolitical borders and other places of culture contact—establish themselves as owners of Mexicano exhibitions. A sense of ownership is particularly evident during the opening night of an exhibition, when museum members, artists, and community leaders are invited to an evening reception. I have observed Mexicano visitors act as translators and cultural ambassadors to European Americans and others who are not familiar with the work on display. The tone and stance of the translation are significant. Mexicano museum visitors do not whisper, apologize, or defend the objects but instead speak with confidence and pride as they describe their relationship to the work, its content, and its message. Rarely have I heard self-appointed cultural ambassadors ask for an interpretation from an artist or curator, because in claiming ownership in the work they authenticate their own perspective. That is, these self-appointed cultural ambassadors do not act like docents because they do not tell others what *the* meanings are behind an object. Instead, they convey their own experience and understanding of the object.

These interpretations are not rare as a diverse crowd attends the opening-night receptions at the MFACM, including city officials, diplomats, the Mexican consul, Pilsen and Little Village residents, schoolteachers, students, and working-class families, as well as artists, arts organizers, and arts promoters. A local arts administrator has been known to comment that at the MFACM, especially on opening night, "you never know where you are" since Chicago's racial tension and history of segregation produce monocultural participation at most events, whereas at the MFACM African Americans, European Americans, and Mexicanos are in the same room.

On the weekends Mexicano visitors may not be as vocal in claiming objects as their own, but "mom, dad, and the kids" also make the MFACM a homespace.[56] Families with children often photograph, or increasingly videorecord, objects on display at the Center Museum. Parents often guide their children through exhibits, reading labels, explaining images, and encouraging them to show respect for the MFACM and the objects on display. In fact, the sacredness of the MFACM is signaled by the absence of graffiti and other acts of vandalism, even though many of the surrounding public buildings, stores, and fences in the Pilsen neighborhood are sites of gang-and non-gang-related calligraphy. Substitution of the word "calligraphy" for the word "graffiti" is an attempt to eliminate a political bias or judgment against writing on walls. It is also an attempt to link this type of writing with other types of writing that are equally stylized and enjoy a historical tradition. (See Marcos Sanchez-Tranquilino, "Murales del Movimiento: Chicano Murals and the Discourses of Art and Americanization," pp. 804–811 in Eva Sperling Cockcroft and Barnett-Sanchez, Holly, [Eds.] *Signs from the Heart*: California Murals. Social and Public Art Resource Center, Los Angeles, 1990.)

Making the Center Museum a sacred space also occurs during the annual Día de los Muertos celebration. As stated above, the Day of the Dead is itself a cross-cultural event in that it originates from both pre-Columbian cosmology and European Catholicism. The celebration of the Day of the Dead inside the museum's walls transforms the function of the museum. However, it is the experiences of Mexicanos themselves as they physically encounter ofrendas for the dead which relocate the museum into a sacred place, a place of worship, or a *familia*-centered space. My observations indicate that each of these reconstructions is a claim to ownership and authority in objects and the culture the objects represent.

In 1990, while standing in front of an installation designed by Arturo and José Barrera to commemorate the death of Pilsen's Mexicano youth lost to gang violence, a young woman cried over those she had never met as she remembered her own violent childhood. Her remembrance invoked by the ofrenda works to unite two unrelated experiences. This woman's relationship to the ofrenda is not representative, however, since many museum-goers seek out a particular ofrenda in order to mourn, celebrate, or commemorate a particular life and death. Patricia

Martinez's ofrenda/installation to her fifteen-year-old brother was intended as a sacred site because this high school student and Golden Gloves boxer had been shot to death a few months before the opening of the exhibit. Family and friends made a pilgrimage to her ofrenda in order to honor his life and death. People standing before the ofrenda were storytelling, remembering, and crying. This became a common observation because several ofrendas commemorated the premature deaths of local youth.

I have also observed museum-goers engage with objects in ways that suggest historically based ownership. In 1992 I observed a father and daughter standing in front of a special installation addressing the quincentennial created by Ricardo, Paula, and Miguel Linares. The installation featured papier-mâché figures depicting the violent encounter between the Spanish conquistadors and the indigenous people of Mesoamerica. After a few moments the man turned to his daughter and told her about the times when his own father made papier-mâché dolls for him and his brothers and sisters. Storytelling is a common observation at Day of the Dead and other exhibits because parents use the exhibits as a way to demonstrate to their children practices and events from their own past. Through memories of particular experiences, spiritual connections to images, and the positioning of objects as familiar, Mexicanos move objects into a zone of their own complex, multisubject, personal history and homespace.[57]

I have suggested that mestizaje (a metaphor for experience and analysis) is more instructive than familiar geopolitical boundaries and nationalistic discourse for understanding exhibitions at the MFACM. We do not need to designate Mexicanos, objects attributed to Mexicanos, and actions of Mexicanos as either co-opted or resistant, as either American or Mexican, as either modern or traditional; to do so only flattens experience. Mestizaje is a metaphor that allows us to recuperate the heterogeneous and complex experiences of Mexicanos, to examine the porous and fluid zone of contact, to study the multiple and fractured positionality of the subject. That is, mestizaje allows for the study of the subject itself.

In this late capitalist moment, as museums and other institutions can no longer operate as an apparatus of the nation-state, new coordinates and sites for collective representation must be explored. It is necessary to uncover these new hybrid zones, the unmapped spaces of cultural production that emerge from global reconfiguration. Hybrid spaces, however, are not idyllic; they are rife with conflict and chaos. It is the unresolved conflictive moment that produces originality and creativity, new forms and meanings: mestizaje. Mexicano exhibitions criss-cross and mix techniques of representation and interpretation established by nation-building art and ethnography museums. In the hybrid space the MFACM not only rewrites the narrative of the nation, but allows visitors to reconfigure "the cultural" (and "the national") in ways that are not tied to notions of "us" and "them." Constantly negotiating between cultures, Mexicanos work to create a place that they can call home. The site of their homespace, their bodies, allows them to act as an authority, a familiar, and an expert when they encounter Mexicano exhibitions. Although deterritorialized, Mexicano homespaces can belong only to themselves.[58]

ENDNOTES

1. "Public museum" refers to those large museums that are usually publicly owned or financed in part by taxes and public revenues as well as the privately owned universal survey museum intended to represent the public. See Carol Duncan and Alan Wallach, "The Universal Survey Museum" *Art History* 3 (1980), 448–469.
2. Sally Price, *Primitive Art in Civilized Places* (Chicago: University of Chicago Press, 1989); Carol Duncan, "Art Museums and the Ritual of Citizenship," in Ivan Karp and Steven D. Lavine (eds.), *Exhibiting Cultures: The Poetics and Politics of Museum Display* (Washington, DC: Smithsonian Institution Press, 1991).
3. Gary Kulick, "Designing the Past: History-Museum Exhibitions from Peale to the Present," in Warren Leon and Roy Rosenzweig (eds.), *History Museums in the United States: A Critical Assessment* (Urbana and Chicago: University of Illinois Press, 1989); Lawrence Levine, "The Sacralization of Culture," in *Highbrow/Lowbrow: The Emergence of Cultural Hierarchy in America* (Cambridge, MA: Harvard University Press, 1988), 146.
4. Neil Harris, "The Gilded Age Revisited: Boston and the Museum Movement," *American Quarterly* 14 (Winter 1962), 552–554.
5. Néstor García Canclini, *Transforming Modernity: Popular Culture in Mexico*, trans. Lidia Lozano (Austin: University of Texas Press, 1993), 7.
6. Michael M. Ames, *Museums, the Public, and Anthropology: A Study in the Anthropology of Anthropology* (Vancouver: University of British Columbia Press, 1986), 39.
7. Donna Haraway, "Teddy Bear Patriarchy: Taxidermy in the Garden of Eden, New York City, 1908–1936," in Nicholas B. Dirks, Geoff Eley, and Sherry B. Ortner (eds.), *Culture/Power/History: A Reader in Contemporary Social Theory* (Princeton, NJ: Princeton University Press, 1993).
     Patricia Penn Hilden, Shari Huhndorf, and Carol Kalafatic, "Fry Bread and Wild West Shows: the 'New' National Museum of the American Indian" (unpublished manuscript, 1995), demonstrate how the "new museology" changes very little in the history of interpreting Native American cultures.

Their astute critique of the George Gustav Heye Center of the National Museum of the American Indian illustrates that even "artistic" approaches to Native American objects signify exotic and noble savages.

8. Elinor Bowles, *Cultural Centers of Color: Report on a National Survey* (Washington, DC: National Endowment for the Arts, 1992), 26. More than three-fourths of the arts organizations were formed in the 1970s and 1980s. Only 6 percent were created in the 1960s. Taking a longer historical perspective, minoritized populations in the United States have been producing their own cultural institutions for centuries. For example, African Americans have been creating their own places of worship, education, and celebration since the onset of slavery in the Americas. Mexican Americans have been creating their own music (*el corrido*), forms of worship (*el penitente*), and cultural products (*la santera*) since the annexation of northern Mexico in 1848.

9. Malaquias Montoya and Lezlie Salkowitz-Montoya, "A Critical Perspective on the State of Chicano Art," *Metamorfosis* 1980.

10. Jesús Martín-Barbero, *Communication, Culture and Hegemony: From the Media to Mediations*, trans. Elizabeth Fox and Robert A. White (London and Newbury Park, CA: Sage Publications, 1993). See also García Canclini, *Transforming Modernity*, viii.

11. Alan Knight, "Racism, Revolution, and Indigenismo: Mexico, 1910–1940," in Richard Graham (ed.), *The Idea of Race in Latin America, 1870–1940* (Austin: University of Texas Press, 1990), 84.

12. Ibid., 86.

13. Gloria Anzaldúa, *Borderlands/La Frontera: The New Mestiza* (San Francisco: Spinsters/Aunt Lute, 1987), preface.

14. Ibid., 19.

15. Marcos Sanchez-Tranquilino and John Tagg, "The Pachuco's Flayed Hide: The Museum, Identity, and Buenas Garras," in Richard Griswold del Castillo et al. (eds.), *Chicano Art: Resistance and Affirmation, 1965–1985* (Los Angeles: Wight Art Gallery, University of California, 1991).

16. Ibid., 101.

17. James Clifford, "Four Northwest Coast Museums: Travel Reflections" in Ivan Karp and Steven D. Lavine (eds.), *Exhibiting Cultures: The Poetics and Politics of Museum Display* (Washington, DC: Smithsonian Institution Press, 1991), 225–226.

18. Although there are institutions devoted to the display of Chicano and Mexicano art/culture in nearly every metropolitan city in the Southwest, this paper focuses on the MFACM because it is presently the largest and most financially successful Mexican American museum in the United States. See Davalos, "Chicano Art Exhibition as Border Space," Paper presented at Displacing Borders Conference, American Studies Working Group (Berkeley: University of California, March 22, 1995) for an examination of exhibition practices in San Francisco and Los Angeles. I do not suggest that the midwestern location explains mestizo representational practices; on the contrary, I imply that all Chicano and Mexicano exhibition is informed by mestizo experience.

19. Since there are various ethnic identifiers for people of Mexican descent, a note of clarification is required. Not only have people of Mexican descent historically been categorized in various ways by local, regional, and federal governments, but the population itself has created its own ethnic identifiers throughout history. More important, all ethnic identifiers are a contested terrain, and no one enjoys absolute authority over others. In this chapter, I refer to people of Mexican descent in Chicago as Mexicano. Research indicates that this identifier is employed in everyday conversations and family-centered discussions among Chicago's recent immigrants, Mexican Americans, long-term residents who have not become U.S. citizens, as well as mixed-heritage youth. (See Davalos, "Ethnic Identity among Mexican and Mexican American Women in Chicago, 1920–1991," Ph.D. dissertation, Yale University, 1993.) Following academic convention, the ethnic identifier "Chicano" refers specifically to Mexican American populations in the Southwest.

20. Roland Cardona, *Northwest EXTRA*, September 9, 1987.

21. Interview with Carlos Tortolero, July 8, 1994.

22. Quoted in Jay Pridmore, "Hispanic art making a leap into city's consciousness" *Chicago Tribune*, April 22, 1988, Section 7 p. 42.

23. Michele Nadanyi and Mark Parry, "Case 26: Mexican Fine Arts Center Museum," in Douglas J. Dalrymple et al. (eds.), *Cases in Marketing Management* (New York: John Wiley and Sons, 1992), 317.

24. The disbursement of property tax funds for museums on park property was established in 1838 as a development plan to promote the city's arts institutions. The Chicago Park District is a government body formally separate from the City of Chicago but informally connected in that the mayor appoints its Board of Commissioners. Barbara Page Fiske (ed.), *Key to Government in Chicago and Suburban Cook County* (Chicago: University of Chicago Press, 1989), 143.

25. It is beyond the scope of this study to distinguish between ethnography and history museums. For this study, the important distinction is between museums that inscribe objects as art versus those that inscribe objects as cultural artifacts.

26. Carol Duncan, *Civilizing Rituals* (London and New York: Routledge, 1995), 5.

27. Barbara Fahs Charles, "Exhibition as (Art) Form," in Jo Blatti (ed.), *Past Meets Present: Essays about Historic Interpretation and Public Audiences* (Washington, DC: Smithsonian Institution Press, 1987), 97; Ames, *Museums, the Public, and Anthropology*, 37.

28. Mihaly Csikszentmihalyi and Rick E. Robinson, *The Art of Seeing: an Interpretation of the Aesthetic Encounter* (Malibu, CA: J. Paul Getty Museum and the Getty Center for Education in the Arts, 1990), 17.

29. Ibid., 138.

30. Douglas Crimp, *On the Museum's Ruins* (Cambridge, MA and London: MIT Press, 1993), 15.

31. Ibid., 17.
32. Ibid., 18
33. Barbara Kirshenblatt-Gimblett, "Objects of Ethnography," in Karp and Lavine (eds.), *Exhibiting Cultures.*
34. Sally Price, *Primitive Art in Civilized Places* (Chicago: University of Chicago Press, 1989).
35. The material for this section of the chapter was gathered during five field research periods (May 1990-November 1992, the summers of 1989 and 1994, and brief visits in 1995 and 1996). Formal and open-ended interviews with the MFACM's founders, Carlos Tortolero and Helen Valdez, as well as René H. Arceo Frutos, Encarnación Teruel, and Rebecca D. Meyers, produced a baseline of information. In-depth ethnographic observation and ongoing contact with the Center Museum's staff and administration are supplemented by primary and secondary sources, including materials generated by local media and the Center Museum between 1987 and 1989. Admittedly, the specific exhibitions I discuss do not represent the entire history of the MFACM. I selected examples that are representative of the Center Museum's exhibition goals, are experienced by a large number of people, and are unique in the history of art/culture exhibition.
36. See Tomás Ybarra-Frausto, "The Chicano Movement/The Movement of Chicano Art," in Karp and Lavine (eds.), *Exhibiting Cultures.*
37. Mexican Fine Arts Center Museum, "The Amate Tradition: Innovation and Dissent in Mexican Art," Exhibition brochure, 1995.
38. "Arte y Arte Popular/Art and Popular Art," in Johathan D. Amith (ed)., *The Amate Tradition: Innovation and Dissent in Mexican Art* (Chicago and Mexico City: Mexican Fine Arts Center Museum and La Casa de Imágenes, 1995), 24.
39. Ibid., 24.
40. MFACM, "Amate", Exhibition panels.
41. MFACM, "El Juguete Popular Mexicano/Popular Toys of Mexico," Exhibition materials, 1991.
42. Ibid., "What Is a Toy?"
43. I am indebted to Alex Saragoza for this perspective.
44. Martín-Barbero, *Communication, Culture and Hegemony;* García Canclini, *Transforming Modernity,* especially pp. 42–47.
45. It must be admitted that from a wider perspective, the MFACM does not exclusively recirculate Mexican nationalism. Indeed, the Amate exhibition recognizes the role of the government in stimulating the production and the marketing of amate. Other exhibitions, such as "Latino Youth: Living with HIV/AIDS in the Family" (May 15-June 7, 1992) and "Art of the Other México: Sources and Meanings" (June 18-September 12, 1993), offer a critique of official Mexican culture and nationalism. These two exhibitions subvert the homogenizing effects of nationalism by exhibiting and promoting the identity of groups and peoples not sanctioned by official Mexican culture. More important, Latino Youth does not present the romantic or nos-

talgic image of official Mexican culture but portrays the realities of Mexicano experience.

46. Carlos Tortolero, "Introduction," *Mexico: La Vision del Cosmos: Three Thousand Years of Creativity* (Chicago: Mexican Fine Arts Center Museum, 1992).

47. Laurene Lambertino-Urquizo, "Aztec Ceramics and Colonization," *Mexico: La Vision del Cosmos: Three Thousand Years of Creativity* (Chicago: Mexican Fine Arts Center Museum, 1992), 47; Donald McVicker, "The Field Museum's Collection from México," *Mexico: La Vision del Cosmos*, 65–66.

48. Ames, *Museums, the Public, and Anthropology*, 38.

49. McVicker, "Field Museum's Collection," 65.

50. MFACM, "Mexico, La Vision del Cosmos: Three Thousand Years of Creativity," Exhibition materials, 1992.

51. According to Chicago curator and arts activist Juana Guzman, the phrase does not signify an indigenous voice or an original voice, but instead points to a community's right to interpret itself. Interviews with Juana Guzman, July 1, 1994, and March 29, 1995.

52. MFACM, "Meaning of Día de los Muertos: 500 Years of Resistance," Exhibition materials, 1992.

53. I employ the word "senses" to connote both knowledge and sensory experience.

54. Duncan, "Art Museums and Ritual of Citizenship"; Duncan, *Civilizing Rituals*.

55. The term is a modification of bell hooks's concept of a "homeplace." (See bell hooks, "Homeplace: A Site of Resistance," in *Yearnings: Race, Gender, and Cultural Politics* (Boston: South End Press, 1990).

56. Executive Director Carlos Tortolero frequently refers to the MFACM's audience as "mom, dad, and the kids."

57. Private encounters with public representations also occurred during one of the Center Museum's inaugural exhibitions. According to Tortolero, during "Images of Faith/Imagenes de Fe: Religious Art of Mexico, Eighteenth and Nineteenth Centuries" (March 27–May 13, 1987), Mexicanos reinscribed the MFACM as a place of worship by filling the Center Museum's comments book, a blank book provided for visitors' responses to exhibitions, with testimony about the saints. By giving *testimonio* at the MFACM, Mexicanos reclaimed these otherwise historically and culturally distinct objects as their own personal channel between the sacred world and the secular world. Even though the objects were in a museum, Mexicanos used their own senses to experience the objects in familiar ways.

58. Earlier versions of this chapter have benefited from the comments of Patricia Penn Hilden, Alex Saragoza, Ileana La Bergère, the participants of the University of Illinois Chicago-Colegio de Michoacan Conference, Mexico and Chicago: the Dynamic of Transnational Migration, and the support of Carlos Tortolero and Helen Valdez. I would also like to acknowledge support for writing and research from The Chancellor's Postdoctoral Fellowship at the University of California, Berkeley, in the form of a two-year grant (1994–1996). Of course, the conclusions are my own.

4 THE HIJACKING OF A HERITAGE: THE CALIFORNIA MUSEUM OF LATINO HISTORY—DISCOURSE, POLITICS, AND HISTORY

Antonio Ríos-Bustamante

In this case study Antonio Ríos-Bustamante identifies the interest groups and examines the problematics and rhetoric involved in the efforts to establish a Latino museum of history in Los Angeles. The chapter focuses on the first phase (1984–1987) and second phase (1987–1989) of the ongoing and still unfinished process. Among the issues examined are the politics of museum organization; the choice of private or public museum status; the relationships between museum organizers, politicians, and the community; and the California state museum policy process.

—The editors

The creation and organization of new ethnic museums represents a challenge and an opportunity for the field of public history. The process of forming a new museum includes program development, funding, planning, and the identification of services for new audiences. Latino, Mexican American, Puerto Rican, and Cuban American museums share similar development issues with African American, Native American, and Asian American public history programs. Latino public history programs also reflect the particularities of the various Latino communities. This essay is a case study of the Los Angeles Latino museum formation process from 1984 to 1990, with an update to 1995.

MUSEUM RHETORIC AND POLITICS

Chicano(a) literary scholars have found that nineteenth-and early twentieth-century Mexican American writers employed a dualistic discourse in addressing Anglo and Mexican audiences. This dichotomy resulted in a complex matrix of conscious and unconscious relationships and contradictions, producing a discursive disjunction. The dualistic rhetoric of these authors has recently been described by literary historian Genaro Padilla, who found that the texts conveyed different, often contradictory messages to Anglo and Mexican readers and contained subtextual messages.[1] These contradictions and subtexts reflect the contradictory or subconscious dimensions of the mind-sets of the authors.

Discursive disjunctions have continued and evolved within Hispanic and Mexican American policy discourse and rhetoric. An analysis of language and text can deconstruct the ideas and the subjective and objective meanings within both textual and cultural public policy contexts.

The effort to establish the California Museum of Latino History (CMLH), described here, exemplifies such a disjunctive discourse process. It also demonstrates the importance of different rhetorical styles of language and the meanings underlying the discourse of various types of participants in a cultural public-policy process.

The Latino museum development policy process involved complex public relations that had separate realities for highly varied players. These players included CMLH museum organizers, politically motivated elected officials, the news media, and an underinformed public. Each of these groups was characterized by distinctive rhetorics, mind-sets, behavioral modes, and ethical codes. The following is a case study of the Los Angeles Latino museum development process from 1984 to 1990, examined in the context of a distinctive discourse.

THE BACKGROUND

The establishment of the California Museum of Latino History was the outgrowth of several years of efforts to produce Mexican American historical programs in the greater Los Angeles area. Among these efforts was a series of public history exhibitions,[2] such as the "Social and Cultural History of Mexican Los Angeles, 1781–1881" (see Figure 4.1), an exhibit created for the Los Angeles Bicentennial of 1981,[3] and the "Latino Olympians: A History of Latino Participation in the Olympic Games, 1896–1984."[4] The CMLH museum organizers, Antonio Ríos-Bustamante and William Estrada, subsequently learned about earlier antecedents, such as former Los Angeles City Councilman Edward R. Roybal's idea of establishing a Museum of the City of Los Angeles, which would have emphasized the city's Mexican heritage.[5]

The CMLH organizers were stimulated by the establishment of several new museums, including the Temporary Museum of Contemporary Art, the California Afro-American Museum, the Los Angeles Holocaust Museum, and the National Japanese American Museum.[6] The continuing

Figure 4.1. Two views of the Social and Cultural History of Mexican Los Angeles—1781–1881 in Los Angeles, September 1981. *Photos by Antonio Ríos-Bustamante.*

efforts to organize Italian American, and Chinese American museums also served as models.[7]

MUSEUM CRUSADE

The CMLH organizers' effort to establish a museum began in December 1984, following the broad success of their exhibition "The Latino Olympians: Latin American Participation in the Olympic Games, 1896–1984." The organizers were professors and students of Chicano History rather than politicians.[8]

The CMLH organizers possessed professional expertise in the production of historical programs and exhibits, but with the exception of a few key supporters, they had only limited experience with the state's public policy process. They did gain the much-needed support of a handful of political organizers and activists,[9] which proved invaluable in organizing lobbying efforts and interpreting the actions of elected officials. The experience and advice of the political organizers combined with the energy and enthusiasm of the scholars to launch the campaign for a museum.

An honorary board of directors was established, comprising elected officials, academics, businesspeople, community representatives, and notables. A working board and an auxiliary board of directors were composed of six historians, one health services administrator, two media professionals, and four business people. An advisory council comprising over twenty persons included fourteen academics, four media professionals, and others from all walks of life. Ongoing efforts were made to secure additional participation of businesspeople and political organizers; these met with varying success.[10]

Antonio Ríos-Bustamante, William Estrada, coordinated the core organizational activities, assisted by a large periphery of supporters. Campaign and development plans for the museum outlined objectives and provided a schedule. Letters and announcements were sent systematically to members of the boards, advisory council, legislators, the governor of California, and members of the public. A series of press releases was sent weekly to the news media, state legislators, organizations, and public agencies between 1984 and 1989.[11] The press releases reported on positive new developments, stimulating a mood of constant movement forward to the establishment of the museum. Press release topics included the activities of new supporters, the board, and advisory council; the awarding of grants; the contents of press conferences, hearings, and meetings; the achievement of nonprofit status; the results of feasibility reports and legislation; and the opening of exhibitions.

The press releases proved to be an effective public relations vehicle for stimulating newspaper articles about the museum organizing activities. For several years small articles appeared consistently in major and local newspapers in the southern and northern California districts of key legislators.[12]

A BILL

CMLH organizer Antonio Ríos-Bustamante drafted model legislation based upon an examination of the bill and statute establishing the California Afro-American Museum.[13] The draft bill provided for the establishment of a new California State Museum of Latino History at Los Angeles, with annual funding of $2 million and $9 million for site acquisition and construction of a building. CMLH organizers and supporters approached California state legislators to identify an author for the legislation.[14] They wrote to every Latino member of the California State Legislature to inform them of the museum effort, and contacted most of them personally.[15]

Ríos-Bustamante and William Estrada met with legislators, city council members, board of education members, and prominent community leaders.[16] They held meetings with Councilman Richard Alatorre; State Senator Art Torres, who had authored the bill for the Japanese American Museum;[17] Assemblywoman Gloria Molina's office; State Senators Reuben Ayala and Peter Chacon; and others.

Congressman Edward Roybal, who was about to retire, shared his experience and his commitment to the preservation of the Mexican American heritage. Conversely, some of the most prominent Mexican American legislators who had supported the efforts of Japanese and Chinese Americans to establish museums were cynical or skeptical about the financial, political, and community support for a Latino museum.

Although these Latino legislators supported and even introduced legislation for the Japanese American, Afro-American, and Holocaust Museums, they did not make a Latino museum a high priority on their agendas. The organizers were given name support and told to come back when they had more political and financial backing.

When Monterey Park/Montebello Assemblyman Charles Calderon agreed to sponsor the legislation, the organizers selected him as the author.[18] At a second meeting, however, Calderon informed the organizers of the existence of a rival effort to establish a "National Hispanic Museum," which had sought his support and that of then Assemblywoman Gloria Molina.

Assemblyman Calderon consulted with other Mexican American elected officials and wrote legislation based on the draft bill by Ríos-Bustamante. Calderon also obtained the initial support of Richard Alatorre and Los Angeles County Supervisor Kenneth Hahn. On January 14, 1986, Councilman Richard Alatorre and County Supervisor Kenneth Hahn held a press conference at the Los Angeles County Museum of Natural History to announce that Calderon was ready to submit legislation.[19] Antonio Ríos-Bustamante and William Estrada presented a statement and were photographed with Calderon and Hahn.

RIVAL EFFORT

Meanwhile, the rival effort was being organized by a one-time associate of Ríos-Bustamante and Estrada. Kirk Whisler, publisher of *Caminos Magazine,* and Sandra Soule, a political organizer, announced the formation of a National Hispanic Museum.[20] Whisler had previously collaborated on and publicized the "Latino Olympians Program" that Ríos-Bustamante and Estrada had coordinated, and the magazine had been contracted by Ríos-Bustamante and Estrada to print the youth history booklet *The Latino Olympians: Latin American Participation in the Olympic Games, 1896–1984.*[21]

In early 1984, when the California Museum of Latino History was being incorporated, the organizers had sought the support of Whisler and *Caminos.* The *Caminos* museum project was formulated and announced without any consultation with Ríos-Bustamante and Estrada. According to the *Caminos* proposal, the National Hispanic Museum would be organized along the concept of a "Hall of Fame" of famous Hispanics.[22] Whisler and Soule then approached Hispanic legislators to introduce legislation to support a National Hispanic Museum. For several months it appeared that two different bills would be introduced until Assemblywoman Gloria Molina agreed to co-sponsor the Calderon bill for a California Museum of Latino History.

By January 1986 this rival effort created a public perception of division in the Los Angeles Mexican American/Latino community.[23] Articles in the *Herald Examiner* and *Los Angeles Times* played up the supposed significance of this division.[24] Support by Mexican American legislators for the Calderon bill effectively ended the effort of the National Latino Museum group. Soon afterward, *Caminos Magazine* went out of existence due to financial difficulties.

MUSEUM RHETORIC AND DISCOURSE

Key discursive terminology and symbols used in the museum policy process, press conferences, and newspaper articles included such concepts and terms as the "dream" of a Latino museum; "California Museum of Latino History"; "history," "art," and "museum professionals"; "one-time funding or permanent state support." These key terms were to figure heavily in the public-policy debate, meetings, and hearings.

Museum organizers first spoke of the "dream" of a Mexican or Latino museum as having a history extending from Edward Roybal's dream of a Los Angeles City Museum, back to the involvement of nineteenth-century Mexican leader Don Antonio Franco Coronel in the formation of what became the Los Angeles County Museum of Natural History. Coronel had donated his collection of original California historical artifacts, which became the core of the California and Southwest collection at the Los Angeles County Museum of Natural History. Thus, Antonio Coronel's dream in the 1890s may be identified as the root of the contemporary museum effort.

Almost immediately this concept was appropriated, first by the effort for a National Hispanic Museum and then by Charles Calderon. *Caminos* publicity also spoke of the dream of establishing a National Hispanic Museum. As soon as he introduced legislation to establish a California Museum of Latino History, Charles Calderon spoke of the museum as his "childhood dream."

Another key concept was "California Museum of Latino History." As defined by Ríos-Bustamante and Estrada, this included the idea of a professional California state museum that would be part of the state's publically administered and funded museums. The California Afro-American Museum provided an existing model and demonstrated the practical feasibility. Following this concept would guarantee a quality institution because a state museum would have to be established and administered according to civil service and other professional standards.

The term "Latino" was adopted to avoid any appearance of competition with the already existing Mexican Museum in San Francisco. It was also adopted to reflect the diversity of California's Spanish-speaking population. A major goal was that all Latino groups be represented according to their actual historical presence and contributions. Programming would be proportional relative to the size and length of historical presence of the various Latino groups. In this concept the Mexican American group would receive major representation, based upon its larger contributions to California history. Since 1989 the term "Latino" has been interpreted by the Latino museum board in a manner that does not provide for proportional emphasis on Mexican American history.[25]

Other key terms of discourse were "history" and "art." The CMLH organizers' proposal was that the museum would be primarily a historical museum because there was already one art museum as well as several

major fine arts programs in Los Angeles and in California, while there
was not even one historical institution or program. A historical museum
would meet an unmet need and avoid potential conflict for funding and
programming with existing art museums and programs, such as the
Mexican Museum and Plaza de la Raza.

Soon after the introduction of the bill by Calderon, he and other political leaders began to move away from an emphasis on a history museum to an art museum. After the appropriation of state and Los Angeles
city funds for a feasibility study, City Councilman Richard Alatorre, at a
meeting on August 18, 1988, in his offices, warned that "potential corporate supporters might be threatened by Mexican American history."[26]
At this meeting Alatorre and Calderon stated that the museum should
emphasize art but continue to include history as a part of its program.
When Ríos-Bustamante suggested that two institutions be established,
one for art and one for history, the political leaders rejected the idea as
unfeasible. In effect, the history part of the program was being retained
merely as a token element for political and funding purposes.

The concept of a museum meeting professional standards was emphasized by the museum organizers from the incorporation of the museum
as a nonprofit organization in 1994. The board of directors included
most of the leading Mexican American historians in California. The museum brochure and the 1996 report by the organizers emphasized that
a state Museum would ensure professionalism and professional standards. From 1986 to 1988, in interviews with the press and resulting newspaper articles, the museum organizers emphasized the need for professional standards by comparing the museum legislation to medical
legislation. The analogy was used that, if the state of California established a hospital or medical program, medical doctors would be involved
in the planning and operation of the program. Logically, if the state of
California established a historical museum, professional and civil service
standards would require the involvement of historians and museum professionals in the planning and operation of the museum.

At the August 18 meeting, Alatorre and Calderon expressed their view
that the concept of a state museum was a bad one because it would re-
duce the independence of a Latino museum. They stated that the museum should be established as a private institution that could receive support from the state of California and city of Los Angeles. This would best
guarantee an institution run by Latino community representatives.

Finally, another concept that originated in the California State Legislature and State Parks and Recreation hearings on the bills for the California Museum of Latino History was that of "one-time funding or

permanent state support." In these hearings representatives of the California State Department of Parks and Recreation opposed the idea of establishing another state museum under their department. Their opposition was based upon the idea that the state should not assume the burden of creating additional ethnic museums because many other groups, such as Italian and Polish Californians, would seek the establishment of museums. As an alternative, it was suggested that a one-time appropriation for a private or non-state Latino museum would be fiscally and politically more feasible. It was also stated that this would require less effort on the part of Latino and other legislators to pass the California legislature. The idea of a one-time appropriation was rejected by the museum organizers because it would not be enough to guarantee either the establishment of a museum meeting professional standards or its continued operation.

HIJACKING OF THE BILL

Despite the end of the National Hispanic Museum effort and the demise of *Caminos Magazine,* Assemblyman Charles Calderon used the short-lived rival effort to distance himself from the California Museum of Latino History organizing group.[27] He stated to CMLH organizers that, because of the existence of the rival effort, he needed to distance himself from the CMLH organizers and any rival groups and that they should concentrate on a lobbying campaign to support "his" museum legislation.[28]

On January 6, 1986, Calderon introduced Assembly Bill 2599, which provided for the establishment of an official California Museum of Latino History.[29] He publicly began to refer to the museum as having been his personal dream since childhood. The legislation closely reflected the draft provided by Antonio Ríos-Bustamante and William Estrada. Assembly Bill 2599 was co-authored by twenty other state assembly persons and by nine state senators.[30] The bill was amended nine times and was heard in four committees of the California State Legislature.

The CMLH organizers, with the help of supporters, began lobbying efforts in the state legislature.[31] To provide data for the state, the CMLH group released a feasibility report in April 1986 that examined need, service population, mission, organization, staffing, sites, cost, and architecture and recommended a plan for development in three scaled phases. Copies of the plan were sent to the legislature, governor, state agencies, museums, members of the public, private organizations, and the news media.

Assembly Bill 2599 passed the California State legislature in an amended version and was signed into law by Governor George Deukmejian in September 1986. The bill found that there was a need for a California Museum of Latino History and appropriated $50,000 to fund a development study. The study was to be conducted under the auspices of the California Museum of Science and Industry and submitted to the legislature on or before June 30, 1987.

After the bill passed, Calderon indicated that he felt no obligation to the CMLH organizers and began to claim that the Latino museum was his own original idea, a dream which he had had since childhood.[32] At the same time he felt no compunction about seeking the CMLH organizing group's continuing support for his legislation.

CMLH MASTER PLAN AND DEVELOPMENT STUDY

Development of a master plan continued with limited support from donors. When completed, the plan would include a feasibility report[33] that proposed a scaled-down effort to create a California Museum of Latino History comparable to the California Afro-American Museum. The planned site was next to existing state and county museums located at Exhibition Park in central Los Angeles.

The CMLH organizers had examined several sites including El Pueblo de Los Angeles Historic Park,[34] Elysian Park, City of Commerce, Griffith Park, Whittier Narrows, and Sepulveda Wash and had concluded that the Exposition Park site was the most developed and already attracted a large Latino audience to existing museums located there.[35] The CMLH also continued to seek foundation and private support for its campaign and development program.[36]

The CMLH organizers met with Don M. Muchmore, director of the California Museum of Science and Industry, and his staff several times at the end of 1986 and in early 1987 to discuss the development study.[37] Among the topics explored were the proposed feasibility report[38] and the bidding process for the development study.

Funding for the feasibility study was placed under the California State Parks and Recreation Department and administered by the California Museum of Science and Industry.[39] The contract for the development study was awarded to Economic Research Associates, Florian Martinez Associates, and Joseph Wetzel Associates. Ríos-Bustamante and Estrada participated in the conduct of the study as unpaid consultants and met several times with the ERA planning group, Don Muchmore's staff, and

Charles Calderon. The *Museum of Latino History Feasibility Study* was completed in May 1987 and transmitted to the governor and legislature in June 1987.[40] The study findings recommended the establishment of the museum without recommending a specific site.[41] As a result of the study, Calderon drafted new legislation.[42]

MUSEUM POLITICS

On January 15, 1988, Calderon introduced A.B. 2798, which provided for the establishment of an official California state-supported museum of Latino history.[43] In April 1988, A.B. 2798 passed the Assembly Committee on Water, Parks, and Wildlife and was sent to the Assembly Ways and Means Committee. It remained in committee until the adjournment of the legislature at the end of 1988. The death of the bill reflected state fiscal difficulties and the opposition of Governor Deukmejian and other interests, including the State Department of Parks and Recreation, which opposed the creation of the museum under its jurisdiction.

With legislation in progress, other players sought to influence the Latino museum discussions. Proposals were advanced to establish the Latino museum at the Southwest Museum, which was experiencing financial difficulties.[44] Most of the existing state agencies and museums appeared to be opposed to state funding, with the California Department of Parks and Recreation consistently indicating its opposition to the establishment or funding of a Latino museum within its administrative jurisdiction[45] Some officials apparently feared that establishing a new state museum could diminish appropriations for other existing and proposed state museums. A number of Latino political leaders indicated that if the museum were established, it should fall within their jurisdiction or district. The museum would thus be a political plum for whoever won it.

The organizers and their supporters repeatedly met with Calderon and sought his restatement of commitment to the original vision of the museum. When it became obvious that Calderon had abandoned any real commitment to the original plan, Antonio Ríos-Bustamante wrote to him on December 23, 1988, on behalf of the CMLH board of directors, requesting that he author no museum legislation in 1989. Instead, the CMLH organizers proposed that the entire Hispanic Caucus, including Calderon, introduce legislation to be authored by another member of the legislature.[46] In spite of this clear statement by the CMLH, Calderon continued to author legislation, and the focus of museum legislation shifted to suit various politicians' interests.

Because of their narrow interests, certain politicians also shifted the emphasis of the museum at this time. Some stated their fear that "Chicano history" could be viewed as "threatening" by corporate interests. They apparently knew little about Mexican American history beyond the holidays of Cinco de Mayo and Sixteenth of September. They felt that an emphasis on art would be more appropriate than an emphasis on history, about which they knew almost nothing.

ENTER THE CITY OF LOS ANGELES

In January 1989 Los Angeles City Councilman Richard Alatorre introduced a City Council resolution to appropriate $50,000 in funds to create a nonprofit foundation to oversee a Latino Museum of Art and Culture effort.[47] The Alatorre plan envisioned the Latino museum as a private institution supported by nonstate funds rather than as a California state museum. An independent institution was alleged to be better than one controlled by state regulations and funding. Alatorre called several meetings regarding the museum issue.[48]

NEW ORGANIZING COMMITTEE

At the behest of Councilman Alatorre, newly appointed City Arts Director Al Nodal acted as a intermediary in bringing the different elements together.[49] On February 21, 1989, Nodal met with Ríos-Bustamante and William Estrada to draft a memo on "The Latino Museum Statement of Purpose and Objectives."[50] The formation of an inaugurating board occurred in March 1989,[51] and its first meeting was held on April 17, 1989.[52] Members of the board included Antonia Hernandez, president of the Mexican American Legal Defense and Educational Fund (MALDEF); Councilman Mike Hernandez; Councilman Richard Alatorre; Councilwoman Gloria Molina; and private attorney Andy Camacho.[53] The CMLH organizers were asked to nominate two members to serve on the inaugurating board. They nominated Dr. Juan Gomez-Quiñones, professor of history at UCLA, and Dr. Arturo Madrid, president of the Tomas Rivera Center.[54]

The inaugurating board formed a new nonprofit entity, the Latino Museum of History, Art, Culture.[55] Because of the similarity of names between the new entity and the CMLH, the inaugurating board was required by the California Secretary of State's office to obtain the written consent of CMLH organizers before filing articles of incorporation.[56] Antonia Hernandez of MALDEF was elected president of the Latino museum board. The new board took steps to employ a consultant to coordinate their efforts[57] and selected David de la Torre, former director of the Mexican Museum, as consultant-coordinator.[58] In the fall of 1989, Assemblyman Charles Calderon was also added to the board.[59] Office space was provided at the MALDEF Los Angeles office.[60]

In April 1990 "The Latino Museum: Short and Long Range Plan 1990–1995" was developed with support from the City of Los Angeles Cultural Affairs Department.[61] Its objectives were stated in the introduction:

> As the Latino Museum becomes established in the 1990s it is anticipated that the institution will fulfill an increasingly important educational role for the Los Angeles area. Recent studies indicate that there are approximately a dozen Hispanic museums in the United States, who maintain strong ties to their communities. These institutions are characterized as being underfunded with inadequate facilities and limited staff. On a national scale, therefore, the Latino Museum's ultimate institutional goal will be to overcome historic patterns in this regard and to emerge as a leader from the beginning in terms of quality programming, scholarship, research and information made available to the general public. Moreover, the Latino Museum will ultimately provide professional training in specific history and art disciplines through internship and volunteer program opportunities. The planning document which follows is the immediate implementation strategy for the short-and long-term functioning of the new museum.

POSTSCRIPT

In 1990 David de la Torre resigned to take another position, and the board announced a search for a new director. Frank Cruz, a former television news anchor and administrator, was hired as executive director.[62] Cruz developed an ambitious plan to establish the Latino museum, predicated on acquisition of a major site. Negotiations were begun with the Lawry Company for a site at the company's 300-acre Descanso Gardens complex.[63]

Efforts were made to persuade a major bank to underwrite a loan to acquire the Lawry site. The costs of acquisition were variously quoted as from $16 to $40 million dollars for the 300-acre site. The negotiations were unsuccessful because of the high cost and lack of funding. After pursuing this ambitious site acquisition, Frank Cruz resigned in 1992 to become chairman of the board of a Latino insurance company, the Gulf Atlantic Life Insurance Company.[64]

The board of the Latino museum initiated a search for a new director but ultimately decided not to fill the position but rather to seek a lower-level coordinator. In 1993 Dennis Acosta Fergusson was hired from the

East Coast to fill the coordinator position. Continuing efforts were made to identify a site and facility to acquire.

CMLH RESEARCH ENTITY

The CMLH has continued to produce historical programs. Committed to continuing their contributions, CMLH organizers Ríos-Bustamante and Estrada decided to change their focus to the development of historical programs.[65] Their efforts have emphasized research on Latinos in museums, the production of historical programs for museums, the identification of historical sites, and educational programs, including research reports, video documentaries, and historical exhibits[66] (for a description of these programs, see "Latino Public History Programs, 1970s-1990s" by Antonio Ríos-Bustamante). They have produced video documentaries such as "Images of Mexican Los Angeles" and the two-part "Latino Hollywood: History of Latino Participation in the Film Industry, 1911–1940" and "Latino Hollywood: History of Latino Participation in the Film Industry, 1940–1990s." Their historical exhibits include "Images of Mexican Los Angeles Exhibit 1781–1990s," the "Latino Olympians Exhibit: A History of Latino Participation in the Olympic Games," and the "Ernesto Galarza" exhibit.[67]

SIN FIN/WITHOUT END

In April 1995 Dennis Acosta Fergusson resigned as coordinator and Denise Lugo was appointed temporary director. In that year the Latino museum obtained a site and facility in an old bank branch building in downtown Los Angeles. Planning and development are underway to develop and open an art program, presumably in this facility.[68] State Senator Charles Calderon stated the intention to open a downscaled program, provided that funding for purchase of the site and for operations became available. As of September 1995, however, there were no funds in hand either for the renovation of the building or for operations.[69] On February 15, 1996, the Latino Museum of History, Art and Culture held a dedication ceremony at the museum site. It was reported that "despite Wednesday's dedication, the museum will not host its first show until at least this fall [1996], and possibly not until next year, once renovation work is complete."

Thus, eleven years after the 1984 effort began, Los Angeles still has no Latino history museum. The Latino museum policy process exemplifies the establishment of a regime of truth by Latino politicians seeking to maintain domination over Latino culture and images in order to control, sanitize, or suppress public interpretations of Latino/Mexican American history. Regarding the site, the *Los Angeles Times* stated, "The museum had originally planned to purchase the building, but the bank is now providing the 40,000-square-foot property in a 15-year, $1 per year lease arrangement."[70]

The Latino museum represents a potential new symbol or icon, the control of which may legitimize interpretations and cultural programs. The Latino museum policy process represents a cultural battle of opposed perspectives and discourses regarding the content and objectives of a Latino museum. Latino politicians fear Chicano/Mexican American history's potential to deconstruct traditional stereotypical history and educate a Latino and general public. "Fine art" is mistakenly viewed as "safe," limited in appeal to elitist and/or controllable audiences.

Los Angeles Mexican Americans, Latinos, and all Angelinos can thank their elected leaders for sidetracking an effort that could have established a basic historical museum program that would have grown. Los Angeles might today be the home of the California Museum of Latino History rather than home to an inaugurating board that, after more than six years, has yet to inaugurate anything.

ENDNOTES

1. Genaro Padilla, *Our History, Not Yours: Mexican American Autobiography* (Madison: University of Wisconsin Press, 1994).
2. Antonio Ríos-Bustamante, "El Orgullo de Ser, Latino Public History: Applied History Programs, Exhibitions and Museums," Working paper no. 17 (Tucson: University of Arizona, Mexican American Studies & Research Center, November 1990).
3. Virginia Escalante, "Photo Exhibit of L.A.'s Latino Legacy," *Los Angeles Times*, September 16, 1981.
4. Virginia Escalante, "Exhibit to Commemorate Contributions of Latino Athletes on U.S. Olympic Teams," *Los Angeles Times*, June 6, 1984; "Latino Olympians Exhibit to Continue," *Los Angeles Times*, September 7, 1984.
5. Conversation of Congressman Edward R. Roybal with Antonio Ríos-Bustamante and William Estrada, 1985.
6. Japanese American National Museum, vol. 3, no. 3 (Fall 1988). Marc Haefele, "Whose Museums?" *L.A. Reader* 9, no. 23 (March 27, 1987). "A Wider Victory," Editorial, *Los Angeles Times*, September 23, 1985. Laird Harrison, "$750,000 Bill Signed for Nikkei Museum" *Asian Week* 7, no. 6 (September 27, 1985).
7. Nancy Graham, "Corporation to Promote Hollywood Expo: Roberti, Woo to Lead Museum Group," *Los Angeles Times*, October 31, 1985.
8. Articles of Incorporation of the California Museum of Latino History, Oc-

tober 17, 1984. "The California Museum of Latino History," brochure, 1985. CMLH Annual Reports, 1984, 1985, 1986, 1987, 1988. CMLH Statement, "A State Mandated Museum," 1985. CMLH, "CMLH Feasibility Report," April 1985. Antonio Ríos-Bustamante, "What the California Museum of Latino History Can Do and Why," 1985.

The primary organizers of the museum were historians Antonio Ríos-Bustamante, executive director; William D. Estrada, assistant director. Major supporters included Dr. Juan Gomez-Quinoñes, Dr. Carmen Carrillo, Dr. Luis Leobardo Arroyo, Antonia Castañeda, and businesspersons Elmira Gonzalez, Ernesto Collosi, and Dennis Melendez. Additional supporters included Ray Gonzalez, William Mason, and Thomasina Reed. The board of directors consisted of Manuel Caldera, Dr. Carmen Carrillo, Dr. Pedro Castillo, Dr. Antonio Ríos-Bustamante (president), William D. Estrada (vice president), Dr. Juan Gomez-Quinoñes, Dr. Albert Camarillo, and Dr. Luis Leobardo Arroyo.

Politicians and notables comprised the honorary co-chairpersons of the board of directors, including Rep. Edward R. Roybal, Rep. Esteban E. Torres, Rep. Matthew Martinez, Gov. Toney Anaya, State Sen. Ruben Ayala, Sen. Joseph B. Montoya, Assemblyman Peter Chacon, Assemblyman Charles M. Calderon, Councilman Richard Alatorre, Catherine Machado Grey, Ignacio E. Lozano, Fernando De Necochea, and Don Muchmore. The advisory board comprised twenty-six community leaders from all walks of life. "The California Museum of Latino History," brochure, January 1996.

9. For example, Dr. Carmen Carillo of San Francisco, and Isabel Serna Hernandez of Sacramento and others Lina Doran, "Supporters of Museum of Latino History Still Hopeful of State Funding," *Valley Tribune/News,* June 22, 1986.

10. This included approaching the Association of Mexican American Educators, Latin Business Association, members of the Los Angeles and Oakland Boards of Education, and numerous other groups.

11. From 1984 to 1987 over a hundred press releases were issued to the press by the California Museum of Latino History.

12. The publications that published articles regarding the museum included the *Los Angeles Times, Los Angeles Herald Examiner, San Francisco Chronicle, San Francisco Examiner, Long Beach Telegram, San Jose Mercury, San Diego Union Tribune, Oakland Tribune, Sacramento Bee, El Hispano, Monterey Park Comet, Santa Monica Evening Outlook, San Gabriel Sun, East Los Angeles Sun, La Opinion, La Tribuna del Pueblo, Caminos Magazine, Americas 2001,* and *Fresno Bee.*

13. The bill was introduced by Sen. Maxine Waters and cosponsored by Sen. Art Torres.

14. "L.A. Museum would Honor Contributions of Hispanics," *San Jose Mercury News,* December 25, 1985. Letter from Charles Calderon to Antonio Ríos-Bustamante, December 6, 1984, accepting membership on the advisory council of the California Museum of Latino History.

15. Advisory board members and supporters in Sacramento helped to organize

visits to the offices of California State Legislators by museum organizers and supporters.

16. Los Angeles area Latino politics for the period 1984–1991 and elected officials are discussed in Harold Brackman and Steven P. Erie, "The Once and Future Majority: Latino Politics in Los Angeles," in Abraham F. Lowenthal (ed.), *The California-Mexico Connection* (Stanford, CA: Stanford University Press, 1993), 196–220; Thomas Weyr, *Hispanic U.S.A.* (New York: Harper and Row, 1988), 128–134; and Peter Skerry, *Mexican Americans: The Ambivalent Minority* (New York: Free Press, 1993), 59–90. According to these accounts, Los Angeles Latino politics was characterized by a rivalry between the older political group headed by retiring Congressman Edward Roybal and including Gloria Molina and Lucille Roybal Allard, and Mike Hernandez and the rapidly rising group of Richard Alatorre/Art Torres, variously referred to as the "East Side Machine," "PRI," or "Golden Palominos" and including Richard Polanco, Larry Gonzales, and Lou Moret.

17. State Sen. Art Torres was the author of the bill providing funding for the Japanese American National Museum. Laird Harrison, "$750,000 Bill Signed for Nikkei Museum," *Asian Week* 7, no. 6 (September 27, 1985).

18. CMLH Press Release, October 22, 1985. Letter from Antonio Ríos-Bustamante, "Actions to be taken by Dr. Antonio Ríos-Bustamante, Actions to be taken by Charles Calderon," to Charles Calderon, October 14, 1985. Calderon had begun his political career as an aide to Richard Alatorre. Elected to the California State Assembly in 1982, Calderon had begun to establish a political identity as a conservative Democrat.

19. Marita Hernandez, "Latino Museum Proposal Gains Support," *La Opinion*, January 6, 1986. "Conferencia de prensa," *Noticias del Mundo*, January 14, 1986. "Latino Museum Backed," *Southeast Wave Star*, January 22, 1986. "Latino History Museum Wins Support," *El Sereno Star*, January 22, 1986. "Latino History Museum Wins Lawmaker Support," *Belvedere Citizen*, January 22, 1986. "Latino Museum Proposed," *East Los Angeles Tribune*, January 22, 1986.

20. "The National Hispanic Museum: A Dream Becomes a Reality" *Caminos Hispanic Conventioneer*, 1985; "The National Hispanic Museum: A Plan for the Dream to Become a Reality," stamped received October 19, 1986.

21. Antonio Ríos-Bustamante and William Estrada, *The Latino Olympians: Latin American Participation in the Olympic Games, 1896–1984* (Los Angeles: Latino Olympians Project, 1984). This booklet (funded by contract with the Los Angeles Olympic Organizing Committee) was printed in an edition of 50,000 copies and distributed free of charge to elementary, junior, and senior high school students.

22. "The National Hispanic Museum: A Dream Becomes a Reality," *Caminos Hispanic Conventioneer*, 1985; "The National Hispanic Museum: A Plan for the Dream to Become a Reality," n.d.

23. Ruben Castañeda. "Hispanic Leaders Push for Mexican History Museum," *Los Angeles Herald Examiner*, January 10, 1986.

24. "El Pueblo Unido," Editorial, *Los Angeles Herald Examiner*, January 17, 1986.
25. "She says the museum will intend to unite Latinos, and not just focus on the dominant Mexican heritage. 'They were Mexicans, but they were also Chileans, and other Latinos,' said Hernandez." Antonia Hernandez, president of the board of the Latino museum, quoted in Steven Wolf, "Cultural House Hunting: Latino and Chinese American Museums Finding Permanent Sites," *Downtown News*, 8.
26. Letter from Councilman Richard Alatorre to Antonio Ríos-Bustamante, July 20, 1988: invitation to participate in meeting to discuss museum on August 18, 1988.
27. *Caminos Magazine*, the nonprofit organization proposing the National Latino Museum, also went out of existence at this time. It appears that the rival effort may have been motivated by the need to subsidize the magazine. The proposed "hall of fame" format of the National Hispanic Museum in essence continued *Caminos*'s coverage of prominent Hispanic personalities.
28. Calderon suggested that other groups might also be interested in forming the museum and that he as a legislator needed to be open to all interests. Calderon's actions parallel the analysis of Peter Skerry, a University of California Los Angeles professor of political science, author of *Mexican Americans*. In Chapter 3, "Los Angeles: Moving In, Out and Up," Skerry describes the favorite tactic of Hispanic elite network politicians of using single-issue activists by becoming intermediaries between their issues and the Los Angeles establishment. According to Skerry, most of the Mexican American and Hispanic players in Los Angeles politics, including the "East Los Angeles Machine" elite network politicians, have no real community base of support. Politicians and activists alike depend on activist single-issue politics. Typically, politicians need activists to do the organizational and publicity campaign on issues because they have no grassroots base of support in the Mexican community districts they represent. As in the Steve Rodriguez campaigns for the recall of Art Snyder, elite network politicians have stolen issues from the activists initiating them.
29. Letter from Charles Calderon, February 19, 1986, regarding introduction of A.B. 2599. Norma Aquino Rather, "Un Museo de Historia Latina en Los Angeles," *La Opinion*, June 4, 1986. "Se Establece Museo Latin," *Noticias del Mundo*, June 6, 1986.
30. Assembly members included Art Agnos, Tom Bane, Tom Bates, Robert Campbell, Peter Chacon, Steve Clute, Gray Davis, Gerald Eaves, Wayne Grisham, Teresa Hughes, Phillip Isenberg, Richard Katz, Johan Klehs, Gwen Moore, Jack O'Connell, Steve Peace, Michael Roos, John Vasconcelos, Frank Vicencia, and Maxine Waters. State senators included Ruben Ayala, Art Torres, Joseph Montoya, Paul Carpenter, Wadie Deddah, Dan McCorquodale, Alan Robbins, Herschel Rosenthal, and Edward Royce.
31. Resolution No. 65–13A8, Support for the California Museum of Latino History, Adopted at the regular board meeting held on May 27, 1986. Resolution No. 919, California Museum of Latino History, Alameda County Board

of Education. Resolution Hispanic Advisory Council, California Department of Parks and Recreation, August 8, 1986. Resolution Los Angeles Unified School District Board of Education, March 3, 1986. Resolution California Museum of Latino History, Board of Education, Alhambra School District, Alhambra, California, April 15, 1986. A statewide petition was circulated by CMLH supporters, Petition for CMLH, April 2, 1986. The petition included a cut-out blank form that supporters could mail to the governor.

32. See Martin T. Dee, "Museum of Latino History Looking for Home, State, Status and Funding," *Los Angeles Times*, September 10, 1987.

33. Antonio Ríos-Bustamante and William Estrada, *The California Museum of Latino History: A Feasibility Report*, Preliminary description of space requirements: Museum Building, August 1986.

34. Now El Pueblo de Los Angeles Historic Monument.

35. By 1986 as much as one-fourth to one-half of museum attendance at Exposition Park Museums consisted of Latino families. The California Afro-American Museum reported that one-fourth of its attendance was composed of Mexican Americans and Central Americans.

36. CMLH, "The 1986 Development Campaign: A Prospectus." Efforts were made to seek support from private donors, including businesspeople.

37. CMLH, Annual Report, 1987.

38. Ríos-Bustamante and Estrada, *CMLH Feasibility Report*. Letter from J. Rounds, chief curator, California Museum of Science and Industry, to William D. Estrada, vice president, California Museum of Latino History, January 5, 1987.

39. California Museum of Science and Industry, "Request for Proposals for a Feasibility Study of the California Museum of Latino History," 7 pp., 1986. Letter from David Bibas, California Museum of Science and Industry, to Antonio Ríos-Bustamante regarding draft of RFP, October 27, 1986.

40. Economic Research Associates, Florian Martinez Associates, J. Wetzel Associates, "Museum of Latino History Feasibility Study," May 1987. Letter, April 30, 1987, from Antonio Ríos-Bustamante to J. Rounds, chief curator, California Museum of Science and Industry.

41. Martin T. Dee, "Museum of Latino History Looking for Home, State Status and Funding," *Los Angeles Times*, September 10, 1987.

42. Rodolfo Acuña, "In '88, Latinos Must be Vigilant, and Not Forget," *Los Angeles Herald Examiner*, January 1, 1988. Rodolfo Acuña, "Power Grabbers Threaten Dream of Latino Museum," *Los Angeles Herald Examiner*, January 28, 1988.

43. Assembly Bill 2798, January 15, 1988. Allan Parachini, "Latinos in California: A Cultural Heritage in Search of a Museum," *Los Angeles Times*, January 17, 1988. Subject: California Museum of Latino History, Date of Hearing, April 6, 1988, A.B. 2798, Assembly Committee on Water, Parks and Wildlife. Antonio Ríos-Bustamante, "Coming to Los Angeles: A Museum of Latino History in the United States," *Long Beach Press Telegram*, March 31, 1988.

44. The Southwest Museum was at this time entering a state of financial crisis

that threatened its very existence. Its director was soon to resign because of malfeasance and misappropriation. Suggestions to this effect by Sen. Art Torres and California State University Chancellor Ann Reynolds were viewed by some as an expedient to save the Southwest Museum. Rodolfo Acuña. "Power Grabbers Threaten Dream of Latino Museum," *Los Angeles Herald Examiner,* January 28, 1988.

45. Copy of letter from Henry R. Agonia, director, California Department of Parks and Recreation, to Charles M. Calderon (undated) regarding agency opposition to A.B. 2798. "Though the concept of a Latino Museum is commendable, the department is opposed to this legislation." Bill Analysis A.B. 3084, April 22, 1986, Department of Parks and Recreation.

46. Letter, December 23, 1988, from Antonio Ríos-Bustamante to Charles M. Calderon.

47. Victor Valle, "Issue of Latino Museum Clouds as City Mulls Funding," *Los Angeles Times,* March 30, 1989. Rodolfo Acuña, "Power Grabbers." Council Agenda, City of Los Angeles, April 7, 1989, Item No. (17)3.a, "Approve support of new project entitled Latino History Museum."

48. Letter from Councilman Richard Alatorre to Antonio Ríos-Bustamante, July 20, 1988: invitation to participate in meeting to discuss museum on August 18, 1988. Memo, October 11, 1989, to Friends of the Latino Museum of History, Art and Culture, from Richard Alatorre, Re: Good News State appropriation of $300,000 for startup, appropriation of $50,000 in City of Los Angeles funds.

49. Memo from Adolfo Nodal, general manager, November 29, 1988, to Finance and Revenue Committee, Subject: Cultural Affairs Department Report . . . and Los Angeles Latino History Museum.

50. Memo from Al Nodal to Councilman Richard P. Alatorre, Subject: The Latino Museum Statement of Purpose and Objectives, February 21, 1989. Members of the inaugurating board were nominated two each by Alatorre, Molina, and by Ríos-Bustamante and Estrada.

51. Memo from Richard Alatorre to Charmay Allred, cc: Antonio Ríos-Bustamante et al., Re: Inaugurating Board for the Creation of a Latino Museum, March 21, 1989

52. Memo from Adolfo Nodal to Latino Museum of History, Art & Culture Executive Board of Directors, March 27, 1989.

53. Ibid.

54. Memo from Al Modal to Richard Alatorre, Subject: The Latino Museum Statement of Purpose and Objectives, February 21, 1989. Memo to Robin Kramer, chief of staff, Councilman Alatorre's Office, Subject: Nomination for Latino Museum Board, February 28, 1989.

55. Ibid.

56. Letter from Edward L. Kunkel, attorney at law, to Antonio Ríos-Bustamante, Re: Latino Museum of History, Art and Culture Articles of Incorporation Filing, June 20, 1989.

57. Memo from Mike Hernandez, board member, Latino Museum of History,

Art, Culture to "All Interested Parties," Subject: Announcement of Latino Museum Consultancy, August 16, 1989.

Notice from Antonia Hernandez to Latino Museum Board Members, Re: Meeting 9–30–89. Memorandum from Antonia Hernandez to All Members of the Board of the Latino Museum Art, Culture and History, Re: Process for Retaining Service of a Consultant, June 15, 1989,

58. Letter to Antonio Ríos-Bustamante from Antonia Hernandez, October 2, 1989. De la Torre previously served as director of the Mexican Museum in San Francisco and resigned as a result of disagreements with the board.

59. Letter to Antonio Ríos-Bustamante from Antonia Hernandez, October 3, 1989.

60. Memo from Antonia Hernandez to Latino Museum Board Members, January 27, 1990 Meeting.

61. "The Latino Museum: Short and Long Range Plan 1990–1995" April 1990.

62. Suzanne Muchnic, "Frank Cruz, Caretaker of the Latino Museum Dream," *Los Angeles Times*, February 27, 1991, F4. Letter to National Latino Museums survey, from Alice G. Martinez, September 1991: "Gentlemen: Our Museum is in the formative stage, currently negotiating for a site. Staff consists of 2 persons, a President and Executive Director and an administrative assistant. The information that we contribute to your survey is therefore very scarce."

63. Shauna Snow, "Latino Museum-in-Progress Losses Chief," *Los Angeles Times*, February 8, 1993.

64. Ibid.

65. Ríos-Bustamante in 1989 took a position at the University of Arizona, where he is now an associate professor. William Estrada left his position as assistant dean of students at Occidental College in order to complete his Ph.D. in history at UCLA.

66. Research includes the studies conducted by Antonio Ríos-Bustamante: "El Orgullo de Ser, Latino Public History: Applied History Programs, Exhibitions and Museums," Working paper no. 17 (Tucson: University of Arizona, Mexican American Studies & Research Center, November 1990) and "The National Survey and Directory of Latinos and Native Americans in Museums."

67. "Images of Mexican Los Angeles" and "Latino Hollywood: History of Latino Participation in the Film Industry" were produced and directed by Antonio Ríos-Bustamante. "Images of Mexican Los Angeles" is distributed by Madera Cine Video, Madera, California. "Latino Hollywood" is distributed by Cinema Guild, New York, NY.

68. Jon Regardie, "Casa Sweet Casa: Latino Museum Comes Closer to Finding a Home," *Los Angeles Downtown News* 24, no. 18 (May 1, 1995), 5–6.

69. Suzanne Muchnic, "Latino Museum Finds a Home," *Los Angeles Times*, June 24, 1995. Calderon stated that $600,000 would be required to purchase the site from the Bank of America, with $300,000 each sought from the Los Angeles City Council and the Los Angeles County Board of Supervisors. The organizing committee, which started with $450,000 in 1989, was said to have

a total of $130,000 in pledges and in cash as of June 24, 1995. Additional funds would be required to pay for renovation and for operations. The museum has one full-time employee, Denise Lugo, an art historian who trained in museum studies at the University of Southern California.

70. Patrick J. McDonnell, "Latino Museum's Official Launch an Upbeat Affair," *Los Angeles Times*, February 15, 1996.

5 THE NATIONAL LATINO GRADUATE TRAINING SEMINAR

E. Liane Hernandez

Graduate student Eula Liane Hernandez examines the experience of young Latino scholars attending the summer 1995 Latino Graduate Training Seminar (LGTS) sponsored by the Inter-University Program in Latino Research (IUP) and the Smithsonian Institution's Center for Museum Studies. The Center for Museum Studies was the site of the three-week seminar, at which fifteen young scholars participated in a dialogue that brought together museum professionals and university scholars. The central objective of the annual LGTS is to address and perhaps to redress the Smithsonian's neglect of the Latino population of the United States. The seminar is one of the results flowing from the findings of the 1994 report Willful Neglect: the Smithsonian Institution and U.S. Latinos, *written by the Smithsonian Institution Task Force on Latino Issues.*

—*The editors*

What does it mean to represent? How do we come to represent ourselves? Whose voices are heard and whose are muffled? What role do I play in the construction of meaning and identity? Finally, how does this meaning become fixed for distribution and consumption within a museum context?

Questions like these inform who I am as a Chicana scholar and help to form the backbone of my academic, political, and social life. In the summer of 1995, I was a participant in the second annual Latino Graduate Training Seminar in Qualitative Methodology. In the seminar these questions were articulated and addressed by my colleagues and me, and for us they took on some of their most profound forms.

The Latino Graduate Training Seminar (LGTS) was sponsored by the Inter-University Program in Latino Research (IUP) and the Smithsonian Institution's Center for Museum Studies. The Center for Museum Studies was the site of a three-week seminar for fifteen up-and-coming scholars to meet, discuss, debate, and begin to critically analyze the issues of representing Latino culture(s). We were selected from a nationwide pool of applicants to participate in what Ford Fellow and 1994 LGTS alumnus Jonathan Yorba has called "a national dialogue that bridges museum professionals and university scholars." The central tenets of the annual LGTS are to address and perhaps to redress the situation by which the "Smithsonian almost entirely excludes and ignores the Latino population of the United States."[1] The 1994 report *Willful Neglect: The Smithsonian Institution and U.S. Latinos*, written by the Smithsonian Institution Task Force on Latino Issues, raised many of the central questions that we examined during the seminar.

The report found that the Smithsonian's failure to reflect the contributions made by U.S. Latino populations via collections and exhibitions has caused two-fold damage: it has denied Latinos claim to a U.S. heritage while also perpetuating the myth that Latinos have not contributed to U.S. culture and history. One need not look far to see that this mentality is part and parcel of a contemporary North American mind-set. It is a particularly troubling predicament for Latino because of the tremendous international influence that the Smithsonian Institution carries as both the nation's largest museum complex and, to quote our final report to Secretary Ira Heyman, "the symbolic repository for U.S. culture and history." This authoritative position is reinforced by the museum's location in Washington, D.C., which carries ramifications that resonate on the national and international levels.

Establishing a Latino presence in the institution is paramount. The Task Force report identified five specific areas—governance, personnel, collections (including acquisitions research and exhibitions), programs (including education and public programming), and budget—as areas in which Latinos are underrepresented in the Smithsonian. Underrepresentation in governance, where Latinos represent less that 2 percent of the collective Smithsonian governing and advisory boards, tends to be self-perpetuating. There is very little outside regulation, a trend that appears unlikely to change. As of 1993 (when *Willful Neglect* was compiled), there existed little evidence of any institutional commitment to change.

The recruitment and advancement of personnel are the greatest challenge; in 1993 the Smithsonian employed 6,553 people. Of this total, Latinos represented 178 employees, or less than 2.7 percent of the total workforce of the Smithsonian, a percentage surpassed by all other racial and ethnic designations, including "other." Additionally, it is important to recognize that the vast majority of this 2.7 percent worked in the security pool. By comparison, African Americans represented 35 percent of the total workforce in a variety of positions.[2]

The participants in the LGTS began a dialogue with employees of the Smithsonian in various departments in order to identify the root of the problems and articulate ways to remedy them. We had an opportunity to meet with Latino employees and gain insights into how the Smithsonian is supposed to function to represent all Americans. In this way I came to understand that the true meaning of the seminar was, as one of my fellow seminar participants stated, not only the Latinization of the Smithsonian but perhaps more important, the Smithsonianization of Latino culture. I was able to bring back to my local community of Tucson a sense of the larger national culture in which we are situated.

Debate has raged for years in the disciplines of art history and museum studies regarding the function and production of the museum. Art historian Svetlana Alpers suggests that there exists a museum effect "of turning all objects into works of art . . . and the museum as a way of seeing," albeit through our own imaging.[3] From treasure house to secular temple, the museum functions in Western society as a vehicle for conveying meaning and thus knowledge. Therein lies its significance to us as museum visitors and aspiring museum professionals. For as another art historian, Michael Baxandall, has suggested, the museum display is a three-fold venture that engages the exhibitor, the artist, and the viewer.[4] The particular objective and/or sensibility of the exhibitors is always mediated by the knowledge that the viewer brings to bear on the exhibit as well as the intention of the artist. The complexity of this interplay cannot and must not be overlooked. The museum in general and the Smithsonian in particular benefit from what Ivan Karp calls the "alleged innate neutrality of museums and exhibitions. It is this very quality that enables them to become instruments of power as well as instruments of education and experience."[5] Thus the exclusion of Latinos is disguised by the museum's face of neutrality.

The museum, unlike other cultural instructions, has the unique ability to articulate identity. As Karp has stated, "Exhibitions represent identity, either directly, through assertion, or indirectly, by implication."[6] When the cultural "other" is implicated, exhibitions tell us who we are and, perhaps most significantly, who we are not. Exhibitions are privileged arenas for presenting images of self and "other." This situation becomes particularly complex when the "we" and the "other" converge to form a hybrid—the museum professional of color.

The complexity of this awkward position, of being both subject and object, became very clear to me as I observed and participated in the LGTS and witnessed the pain and frustration of Chicana and Puerto Rican middle managers and curators. They struggle to mediate the political and social responsibilities of museum work and the (re)presentation—in all of its complexity—of Latino culture and initiatives. They also struggle to fulfill their own professional goals and duties within the hierarchy of the institution. It quickly became clear that these are often two separate and conflicted roles. In his seminar session Felix Padilla suggested that as scholars of color, we assume an insider-outsider position in which we negotiate and translate whatever we define as "our" culture for our community as well as the public at large.

In my view the staff and faculty of color at the Smithsonian, predominately women, engage in this process on a daily basis. What touched and frightened me most was not the process itself but rather the obvious emotional conflict experienced by these women as they faced down the overwhelming institutional power of the Smithsonian.

Of course, the Smithsonian also exemplifies certain instances in which this mediation results in tremendously empowering success. Situated within the predominantly African American community of Anacostia in Washington, D.C., is the Anacostia Museum. In our discussions with the director of the museum, we were privy to details of the work entailed in the exhibition "Black Mosaic." "Black Mosaic" was composed of material culture and ethnic imagery from the local African American community. It was trilingual to address the multiplicity of African American experiences, as represented by Dominican, Haitian, and other diaspora communities and expressed via the collected living voice of its participants. "Black Mosaic" was strengthened by the active involvement of its primary stakeholders. The triumph of the exhibition was the commitment of the Anacostia Museum and its employees to take the time, patience, and energy to ask members of the community the question "What do you want and have that represents you?" Hence, "Black Mosaic" represented a process which valued community meetings, focus meetings, and committed local advisory boards. It also had to value the subtlety of encountering real cultural differences and contrasting cultural values, for example, operating on diaspora time as opposed to institutional time clocks.

"Black Mosaic" illustrates more than the sum of its parts because, beyond its collection and acquisition of material culture, oral histories, educational objectives, and community stewardship, it furthered the development of a long-term commitment between the twenty-seven-year-old Anacostia Museum and the community's redefinition of the museum as a transformative, activist, research-oriented institution and as an institution engaged in popular and often ephemeral culture. Dually, the social issues of survival and the forging of connections between various players within the African American community have resonance here.

We, as Chicanos, can utilize the Anacostia Museum and "Black Mosaic" exhibition as models when encountering the very real and tangible differences that exist within the as-yet poorly defined Latino community. We must also remind ourselves of philosopher Linda Alcoff's warning that the depiction of and ability to speak for and about others is not a neat package. In the process we, like the Anacostia staff, must remember not to be reductive in our practices. In the evaluation and packaging of history and culture, which ultimately is the product of the museum, we cannot be fooled into identifying with a false sense of neutrality, one based simply on our membership in the group and thus our position as spokesperson for the group.

Drawing from the example of the Anacostia Museum, we can begin the process of empowering the Latino community to take part in the decision-making process of museum display and identity formation. We must employ our faith and be resilient in taking on the task of (re)presenting ourselves, despite the pedagogical, political and conflict-ridden context, within a Smithsonian Institution dedicated to the experiences of U.S. Latinos.

The Smithsonian holds within its walls 150 years of collecting, cataloging, interpreting, and fixing of identity and history. At the same time that we engage in a dialogue with the Smithsonian about underrepresentation of Latino culture, we must concede that, as a group, Latinos have not yet established an internal dialogue as to who we are and how we want to represent and interpret ourselves.

My colleagues and I were particularly intrigued by our dialogue on representation and self-interpretation. Our differences were multiple. As a Chicana from Arizona, I was faced with, or rather confronted by, the very different reality of East Coast Latinos, who ranged from Colombians to Chileans, Dominicans to Puerto Ricans, Panamanians, Cubans, and a host of others whose cultural and social experience was radically different from my own. I encountered empanadas filled with meat instead of the sweet fruits that I know and love. There also exists a very different sense of religiosity; for example, I was exposed to the *bot nica*. A final point of contrast is the presence on the East Coast of an international community encompassing a very different set of relationships than those along the Arizona-Sonora border. Through these and countless other differences, I was made aware of the very real and contested arena of Latino consciousness. This area of subjectivity stands before us and challenges our movement. Yet all the LGTS participants seemed to recognize the fundamental necessity of working together to advocate on behalf of Latino initiatives with this institution and beyond.

Finally, the LGTS offered the fifteen of us an opportunity to discuss the use of qualitative methods and strategies of information gathering that we might adapt to our own scholarly work. Rather than merely placing the tools at our doorsteps, the LGTS forced us to consider the implications of our basic professional conflict: how to maintain political agency while also establishing so-called legitimacy of scholarship within our various disciplines. We were reminded by LGTS faculty member and scholar Dr. Antonia Castañeda (University of Texas, Austin) that we must always be aware of the politics of what we do within and outside our work. Drawing from the variety of experiences of the participants, whose disciplines ranged from art history to literature, religious studies, sociology, musicology, medical history, history, history of dress, cultural criticism, women's studies, and media arts, we approached the Smithsonian with the ambitious goal of strengthening the Latino presence in the museum community, even to the point of establishing a Latino museum on the Mall in Washington, D.C.

In one of our seminars, Tomas Ybarra-Frausto stated that "to tell is to struggle against forgetting." I carry these words and ideas with me. I try to tell and retell, in all the complexity that I am able, to pay my respects to the voices, images, and sounds that I carry within me. I remain hopeful that we all came away with a sense of the immense possibilities and responsibilities of our task, should we truly wish to take it on.[7]

ENDNOTES

1. Smithsonian Institution Task Force on Latino Issues, *Willful Neglect: The Smithsonian Institution and U.S. Latinos* (Washington, DC: The Smithsonian Institution, 1994).
2. Figures are drawn from ibid.
3. Svetlana Alpers, "The Museum as a Way of Seeing," in Ivan Karp and Steven D. Lavine (eds.), *Exhibiting Cultures: The Poetics and Politics of Museum Display* (Washington, DC: The Smithsonian Institution, 1990), 26.
4. Michael Baxandall, "Exhibiting Invention," in Karp and Lavine (eds.), *Exhibiting Cultures.*
5. Ivan Karp, "Culture and Representation, in Karp and Lavine (eds.), *Exhibiting Cultures.*
6. Ibid.
7. Although all the participants of the LGTS made critical input, Magdalena Mieri and the Center for Museum Studies were noteworthy in providing vital materials. Especially important to me were the roles of the IUP and Dr. Gilberto Cardenas, Drs. Raquel Rubio-Goldsmith and Antonia Castañeda, my companeras Reina Prado and Rocio Aranda-Alvarado, and Ruth Keffer.

6 CHICANO AND LATINO ART AND CULTURE INSTITUTIONS IN THE SOUTHWEST: THE POLITICS OF SPACE, RACE, AND MONEY

Cynthia E. Orozco

Historian Cynthia Orozco examines the development of Latino art and culture organizations as part of a report to the National Association of Latino Arts and Culture (NALAC), the national Latino cultural advocacy organization. Orozco was one of several scholars who conducted the survey, and her portion emphasized Mexican American institutions in the southwestern states of Texas, New Mexico, Colorado, Arizona, and California. The survey included site visits and interviews with representatives of cultural institutions and museums.

The report revealed that despite the formation of several thousand cultural organizations from 1965 to 1995, most folded, leaving the core of institutions examined in this survey. Orozco examines particular regional politics and the influence of demographics, identifies site and space problems, including the politics of securing space, and discusses the effects of institutional racism and elitism. She concludes with a review of the process of institutionalization of Latino culture.

—The editors

Latino art and culture institutions are numerous and varied. The National Association for Latino Art and Culture (NALAC), an arts and advocacy organization, has identified more than 500 such organizations in the United States and Puerto Rico, including theater companies, cultural centers, media arts groups, museums, print workshops, cooperatives, and presses. Chicano and Latino artistic and cultural expression and production are not new but date back to indigenous societies in present-day Mexico and Spain.

In the present-day United States, especially the Southwest, this expression dates back to colonial artistic practices such as santo-making in New Mexico, theater near El Paso in 1598, and literary works such as Cabeza de Vaca's writings in the 1530s. In the nineteenth century individuals like Antonio Coronel, a mayor of Los Angeles, helped found the Los Angeles County Museum of Natural History.[1] In the twentieth century numerous Mexican art and culture institutions flourished in the 1910–1930 period when the United States received its largest wave of Mexican immigration.[2] The post-depression years witnessed a decline in these activities. A rebirth, or *floricimento,* of Chicano and Latino expression took root in the post-1965 period.[3]

Despite the emergence of several thousand Latino art and culture organizations from 1965 to 1995, most have folded.[4] As the director of Centro Cultural Aztlan in San Antonio, Texas, stated, "Back in 1985 there were thirteen different Chicano/Latino arts organization in the city of San Antonio; now [there are] two."[5] The Tampico Art Center, Pintores de la Nueva Raza, Con Safos, and Centro Cultural del Pueblo were some of the associations that died because of sparse funding. Despite underdevelopment, however, in most localities Latino art and culture organizations continue to proliferate. In Tucson, for instance, over fifty-five culture-based voluntary organizations are seeking to create the Centro Cultural de las Americas, a physical site for La Raza's arts in southern Arizona.[6]

In 1989, in response to the history of colonialism and current underdevelopment of Latina and Latino arts, La Raza organized the NALAC, founded by Pedro Rodriguez (San Antonio Guadalupe Cultural Art Center), Juana Guzman (Chicago Department of Cultural Affairs), P. Gus Cardenas (San Antonio), Linda Lucero (San Francisco, Vanguard Foundation), and Johnny Irizarry (Philadelphia, Taller Puertoriqueño).[7] NALAC's objectives are to

1. be a national advocate for Latino arts and cultural issues;
2. facilitate and encourage the inclusion of Latino arts and culture within the private and public sectors: educational systems, labor, commerce, government, and other relevant systems;
3. work toward a unifying pan-Latino, liberating, and self-defining framework and lexicon;
4. ensure the accurate recognition of the historical contributions and struggles of the Latino community, which predates the creation of the United States.[8]

NALAC has sponsored national conferences in 1992 and 1995, issued a publication, and maintains a newsletter.[9]

In 1995 NALAC obtained a grant from the Ford Foundation to assess the historical and contemporary status of selected Latino arts and culture institutions. NALAC contacted the University of Texas at San Antonio

(UTSA) Hispanic Research Center to undertake the study. Conducted in the summer of 1995, the study surveyed forty-three organizations nationwide, including Chicano, Puertoriqueño, and Latino institutions. It was divided into southwestern and northwestern components, and Julio Noboa, a Puertoriqueño, was hired to conduct the interviews in the Northeast and Puerto Rico, and I conducted those in the Southwest. This chapter elaborates on the qualitative nature of twenty-five site visits I made in Texas, California, Arizona, and Colorado. It represents additional findings outside the official NALAC report published in 1996.

At the time I conducted the interviews, I was informed about Latino cultural institutions as a volunteer and supporter of Mexic-Arte Museum in Austin, founded by Sylvia Orozco and Pio Pulido.[10] Orozco was the director, and as her sister and a volunteer, I had a window into the workings of these institutions. Moreover, I have supported Latina and Latino production of the arts since 1976.

This chapter is divided into several parts. First, the NALAC study is explained and methodology discussed. Second, the founding dates of the southwestern institutions are provided. Third, geopolitics is discussed with reference to the political and economic status of La Raza, as well as locality and region. Fourth, site location and physical space are addressed. Fifth, institutional racism and elitism in funding practices are discussed, and finally, the institutionalization of Latino art and culture is examined.

METHODOLOGY OF THE NALAC SURVEY

For the southwestern part of the survey, NALAC selected twenty-five organizations for qualitative interviews[11] and site visits, located in Arizona, California, Colorado, and Texas. Most of the organizations were founded in the 1970s, although some dated back to the 1960s. None were formed before 1965. Teatro Campesino of San Juan Bautista (associated with Luis Valdez) was the oldest, founded in 1965. Most associations were founded within the context of the Chicano movement. La Peña Cultural Center of Berkeley, however, began as a Latin American support group for Chilean political issues. In San Francisco the institutions reflected the city's multicultural Latino context. Roberto Osorio, an El Salvadoreño, helped found the Mission Cultural Center, left to fight the war in El Salvador, and returned to San Francisco.

The following organizations were included in the study:

Teatro Campesino (1965), San Juan Bautista, California
Centro Cultural de La Raza (1970), San Diego, California

Galeria de la Raza (1970), San Francisco, California
Plaza de la Raza (1970), Los Angeles, California
Self-Help Graphics (1971), Los Angeles, California
Su Teatro (1971), Denver, Colorado
Teatro de la Esperanza (1971), San Francisco, California
La Raza Galeria Posada (1972), Sacramento, California
La Peña Cultural Center (1975), Berkeley, California
Mexican Museum (1975), San Francisco, California
National Latino Communications Center (1975), Los Angeles, California
Xicanindio (1975), Mesa, Arizona
Centro Cultural Aztlan (1976), San Antonio, Texas
Mission Cultural Center (1977), San Francisco, California
Multicultural Education Through the Arts (1977), Houston, Texas
Teatro Bilingue (1977), Houston, Texas
Movimiento Artistico Del Rio Salado (1978), Phoenix, Arizona
Arte Publico Press (1979), Houston, Texas
Guadalupe Cultural Arts Center (1979), San Antonio, Texas
Chicano Humanities and Art Council (1980), Denver, Colorado
Cine Accion (1980), San Francisco, California
Latino Museum of Art, History and Culture (1984), Los Angeles, California
California
Borderlands Theatre (1986), Tucson
Festival Chicano (1986), Houston, Texas
Centro Cultural de las Americas (1990), Tucson, Arizona

Each site was mailed a questionnaire and asked to return it completed. Dennis Medina and Rick Reyna prepared the survey instrument, which asked about the organization's history and mission; the sociopolitical and economic conditions of the contextual environment; development of the organization; current status; funding; governance; management; operations; records; programs; audience; and allies.

The site visit included a tour of the institution's physical space, a taped interview, collection of the institution's documents, preparation of field notes, and photographs of the site and founders, directors, board members, staff, or patrons. The interviews were transcribed, and redactions made. The documents collected included the mission statement, articles of incorporation, general description of programs and the institution, organizational chart, and other pertinent papers.

Tours were conducted of the sites, and field notes taken to record observations of the physical site (i.e., office space and art space). UTSA's

Hispanic Research Center transcribed the tapes while Professor Jeffrey Halley and research assistants prepared the redactions. I wrote the 1995 southwestern report with the assistance of Halley.

NALAC expects to publish its findings in 1997 and expects the study to be "an important contribution to the national dialog on cultural arts policy."[12] In addition, with this project NALAC has founded an archive that houses the interview transcriptions, organizational documents, and photos.

GEOPOLITICS AND DEMOGRAPHICS

To a large extent, the local and regional context determines the status of Latino arts and culture organizations The Southwest has been friendlier to Latino arts than the Midwest or Pacific Northwest. Arte Publico Press, an independent Latino press, was founded in Gary, Indiana, a "depressed area" where "there were no resources" and [it] could not thrive"; its subsequent move to Houston permitted a more supportive environment.[13] States outside the Southwest and Illinois have not witnessed vibrant Latino institutions, although a Latino museum exists in Omaha, Nebraska.

Most of these institutions have received minimal support from the private sector. Latino institutions have little access to foundations or corporate boards, and public funding is determined by city tax structures and arts funding policies. For example, Xicanindio of Mesa, Arizona, founded in 1975, is one of the oldest arts groups but exists in a conservative Mormon community outside Phoenix. No Latinos sit on the city council, and when Xicanindio sought city staff support for funding a permanent space, it was refused. The director noted that "two out of three city staff were against us getting that. . . . I have worked with these people, but yet when it came right down to getting support, we didn't get it."[14] In 1993 El Centro Cultural de las Americas of Tucson tried to obtain the old county courthouse as its site, but the Republican majority on the board of supervisors voted against it.[15]

Demographics have also played a role in funding. The Hispanic population in San Antonio is more than 55.6 percent, 29.3 in Tucson, 39.9 in Los Angeles, and 27.6 in Houston. (Statistics from the U.S. Bureau of Census. *Statistical Abstract of the United States 1996.*) These sizable populations have made it easier to advocate for Latino art and culture. Houston Latinos number over a million, while San Francisco and Denver also host substantial populations. In Sacramento and Berkeley, the populace is smaller. Teatro Campesino has been hindered by its rural location in San

Juan Bautista, California, and financially would have fared better in San Francisco. It is now adding an urban base in San Jose. Despite demographic contexts in which La Raza constitutes a quarter or more of the population, however, there has not been strong support for Chicano/Latino art and culture institutions.

Single-member districts (versus at-large representation) have provided a political context supportive of Latino arts groups. The Guadalupe Cultural Art Center in San Antonio is an excellent example. Before single-member districts in 1977, there was insignificant financial support for over ten Chicano art organizations. The director of the Guadalupe explained, "We began to elect Latinos and that's when funding for the arts began to change because those Latinos began looking at how the money had been previously distributed." This "substantial support of the municipal government" reportedly "is unique to San Antonio."[16] Since then city council members have been key to its support, ensuring that race-based institutions receive more equitable funding. Likewise, Houston institutions such as Teatro Bilingue, Festival Chicano, and the Multicultural Education and Counseling through the Arts (MECA) have all suffered from lack of representation on the city council. Although Houston had more Chicanos and Latinos than San Antonio, support for Latino art was minimal.

Support from key political figures is important. La Raza Galeria Posada in Sacramento garnered the support of a Chicano politico and an organization called Chicanos Organized for Political Action. They helped the galeria obtain a permanent home, a historic Victorian house in downtown Sacramento. In other cities Raza politicians have played pivotal roles, but Latinos remain underrepresented on city councils, and officials have not always been willing to support these institutions if their own positions are tenuous. The director of Houston's Festival Chicano reported, "I have friends who are elected officials who are afraid to rock the boat."[17]

SITE LOCATIONS AND PHYSICAL SPACE

Most institutions are located in the barrio by choice. "We're located in the barrio, deep in the barrio," boasted San Antonio's Centro Cultural Aztlan.[18] Four housing projects are located in its radius and it is housed in a mall with health, legal, women's and migrant services. Others, like Phoenix's Movimiento Artistico Del Rio Salado, are located downtown.

European Americans and the Latino middle class have resisted traveling to the barrios to visit Latino institutions. In Denver, San Antonio,

Los Angeles, and San Francisco, patrons of Latino art must cross into spatially segregated Mexican and Latino residential areas. "A good many people still resist coming to our events or having anything to do with us," reported the Guadalupe Cultural Arts Center.[19]

The status of Latino art and culture institutions is reflected in the politics of space. The significance of space is discussed by intellectual and Chicana art historian Amalia Mesa Baines, a board member of La Galeria de la Raza in San Francisco. Referring to San Francisco's galeria, she said it is "a site, a space, a place, a site of affirmation and a site of struggle."[20]

Obtaining a physical site has typically been a struggle. Before San Antonio's Guadalupe Cultural Art Center located at its present site, other Chicano arts groups had struggled for a site for a decade. A precursor, the Tampico Art Center, was located at a bar called El Gallito. Xicanindio of Mesa, Arizona, and the Chicano humanities and Art Council in Denver currently maintain business offices but have no space for art and culture.

Space is a political entity. Whether or not a community has a Latino cultural center speaks to demographics, politics, and money. The physical space that an institution rents, leases, or owns speaks to its status. The only Latino arts groups that own their facilities are La Peña Cultural Center in Berkeley and Sacramento's La Raza Galeria Posada. Ownership alone does not solve financial woes; both require programming funds.

Other organizations, such as Los Angeles's Plaza de la Raza, San Antonio's Guadalupe Cultural Arts Center, and the Mission Cultural Center in San Francisco, have city leases. But according to the Mission Cultural Center, they have not been provided "the kinds of monies to make major capital improvements," and the center is "severely underfunded by the facility point of view."[21] Centro Cultural de las Americas in Tucson has obtained a lease from the state for a historic home, the Charles O. Brown residence, owned by a Mexican woman and her European American husband, but before the group can occupy it, they must raise $400,000 for renovations.

Still other institutions maintain arrangements with city parks and recreation departments. These include Plaza de la Raza in Los Angeles and Teatro Bilingue and MECA in Houston. In the last few years several institutions have obtained community development grants; these include San Francisco's Mexican Museum, Houston's Teatro Bilingue, and Teatro Campesino which received one in San Jose, California.

Most Latino art and culture institutions are renters. Renters are subject to the whims of owners and fluctuating market values and consequently lack organizational stability. The Chicano Humanities and Art Council in Denver, for instance, noted that, "Instead of selling it [their rental space] to us, they decided to make it into a bed and breakfast."[22] Instability has been a particularly thorny problem in Houston. Three institutions have had a long history of site relocations. Teatro Bilingue explained, "We are not a community center, where you are in somebody else's building and would have to do what they say."[23] Festival Chicano noted, "We have facilities that we have to scrounge around for and fund raise for and the city doesn't help us at all." Festival Chicano and MECA both invested funds in renovating rental space. Festival Chicano "spent a lot of money and effort restoring that theater," a reference to the Venus Theater in Denver's harbor ward.[24] San Diego's Centro Cultural de la Raza obtained its site through collective action and public protest, having to enter into a "confrontation" to obtain its leased building. The center elaborated, "The Group said this time that they would not move, made demands to the city to keep the building. Somebody then called the press and media and chained the doors shut and chained themselves to the door and so it was a struggle."[25] This struggle was for a facility quite lacking in essentials at the time.

Latino art and culture institutions are typically housed in inadequate spaces and in second-rate buildings. San Diego's Centro Cultural de la Raza described its space: "It is a water tent built around 1910, not for human habitation [but] to hold water." This space had no restrooms inside its facility for more than fifteen years. "When the public or staff wanted to use the restroom, one had to exit the building, go to the office, go up a flight of stairs, outside of the building, in the park-like setting. . . . it was a daunting experience, particularly for women."[26] Referring to a previous rental space, Houston's MECA noted, "In a state of the art building you wouldn't have that fire problem" and "that building was a fire trap."[27] The Borderlands Theatre's first location in Tucson was a room in a house rented to artists. Later it was housed in Teatro Carmen, a theater house dating back to the 1940s and later condemned.

Theaters and media arts groups in particular have space problems. Several theaters, such Teatro Campesino of San Juan Bautista and Teatro Libertad, a precursor to the Borderlands Theatre in Tucson, began as street theater. Teatro Campesino's future plans include state-of-the-art theaters in San Jose and the new California State University at Monterey Bay. Of the theater groups, only Su Teatro of Denver had a theater. Media arts groups, such as the Los Angeles National Latino Communications Center and Cine Accion of San Francisco, must rent space to showcase films and videos. No Latino-owned state-of-the-art theater for film exists.

The spaces owned or rented by Latinos are lacking, and conference rooms are almost nonexistent. One director did not have an office or even a partitioned space. Few staff members had their own offices.

INSTITUTIONALIZED RACISM AND ELITISM

Arts and media groups receive public funds to which all taxpayers contribute, among them Chicanos and Latinos, whether immigrants or U.S. citizens. But financial support of art and culture has historically gone to Eurocentric institutions controlled and dominated by European Americans.[28] San Antonio's Guadalupe Cultural Art Center explained, "For all of the years that mainstream institutions received very generous support from all quarters of the public and private sector, we Latinos received nothing or next to nothing."[29]

Art monies are parceled out by local and state boards. The constituency of these boards is important, and until recently they were dominated by European Americans. It is unusual for people of color to be the board majority, and tokenism is common. Houston's Festival Chicano director noted, "They have a minority/majority board, but they use our own people to defend their practices."[30] Another added, "The bottom line is that minorities still are getting discriminated against in funding."[31]

Most funding goes to major organizations like symphonies, ballet companies, and so-called city-wide museums. Houston's Festival Chicano argued that "the majority of the community in Houston doesn't use those venues, doesn't care to go those venues, because they can't afford them."[32] Another called Latino taxpayers' taxes that go to the arts a "a racist tax, because 55% goes to the majors." These larger, white institutions are favored over those controlled by people of color. Latino institutions do not receive equitable funding.

Organizations compete for funds based on their budgets and are granted monies proportional to their budgets. This method of competition systematically favors large-budget institutions, almost all of which are controlled by whites. This process of funding is institutionalized elitism.[33] Borderlands Theatre of Tucson explained: "We have an established artistic record . . . [but] we're still seen as small. . . . They are established and we have been frozen out."[34] San Antonio's Centro Cultural Aztlan also concluded, "When you see their final reports you see that they continue on the trend of the big dollars going to the traditional institutions."[35]

Funding policies disadvantage small-budget organizations. San Diego's Centro Cultural de la Raza noted, "We consistently get [the] highest ranking," but awards are "based upon the size of your budget and that's what you can ask for." In other words, small-budget organizations will continue to receive small awards. The center concluded, "It systematically limits you organization." Teatro Bilingue in Houston also noted this barrier: "Their role is kind of set up against us. . . . instead of being creative . . . we are penalized in that we can't give you a percentage of [our] last budget."[36]

The distribution of local art funds does not usually reflect city or county demographics. According to Festival Chicano, La Raza in Houston constitutes 30 percent of the population but receives only 5.5 percent of the funds. San Antonio's Centro Cultural Aztlan concluded, "So what I'm saying [it] is called? Taxation without representation."[37] Inequitable funding is standard practice and demonstrates institutionalized racism and elitism.

INSTITUTIONALIZATION OF LATINO ART AND CULTURE

Latino art and culture organizations have passed the early stages of development and are more organized and professional today. This represents the institutionalization of Latino art and culture. Houston's Arte Publico Press expressed the typical experience: "The earlier years were characterized by a great deal of idealism and a lack of expertise and a lack of resources. A serious lack of resources, space resources, money, personnel, way overworked staff, trying to figure out how to . . . do everything, not knowing. Having to invent it without having anybody to show you."[38] Reflecting on the past and present, the director concluded, "It is an institution . . . it is no longer a funky, impassioned organization."[39]

Discussing the process of bureaucratization, Sacramento La Raza Galeria Posada noted, "A great transformation of making the change, of being a small organization and thinking on a small scale to trying to think on a bigger scale."[40] It added, "A lot of those people who founded the organization were not professionally trained to run an organization. . . . Sometimes receipts were kept in our pocket and sometimes they were lost, and that's how the organization was run. It was run on trust and barter."[41]

Centro Cultural Aztlan in San Antonio stated: "You know, out of the 17–18 years that we have been in existence, to really say that we have been truly organized has been within the [last] six/seven years." Frustrated with racist and sexist policies and practices, other groups folded. Centro Cultural Aztlan of San Antonio noted, "They didn't have the training or the background of just maintaining the volume of paperwork and reporting and audits and monthly financial statements, and bank reconciliations that the city of San Antonio was requiring."[42] Indeed, most of the institutions were founded by artists, not administrators. Over the years staffs have become more permanent and professional.

These organizations are now permanent institutions. They are institutionalized. It is inappropriate to speak of Latino majors and minors, as all the Latino majors are minors when compared to European American controlled institutions like the Smithsonian Institution or the Museum of Modern Art. Nevertheless, some have larger budgets than others. All are rooted in the Chicano movement or some other movement for self-determination or liberation. They were founded as the collective expression of a people.

Like all social movements, the Chicano movement waned, and institutions remained. For years these institutions struggled, with staff members functioning as virtual volunteers. Today most have permanent staff members, but they are underpaid and largely uninsured. The founding of NALAC suggests a new phase by which permanent organizations can network and assist one another. NALAC expresses the collective will of the Latino arts and culture community; it addresses the needs and interests of Latino art and culture institutions. These include the politics of space, race, and money which constitute the institutionalized challenges of Latina and Latino arts and culture organizations.

ENDNOTES

1. See Antonio Ríos-Bustamante, "El Orgullo de Ser, Latino Public History: Applied History Programs, Exhibitions and Museums," Working paper no. 17 (Tucson: University of Arizona, Mexican American Studies & Research Center, November 1990).
2. For an examination of theater in the period 1910–1930, see Elizabeth C. Ramirez, *Footlights Across the Border: A History of Spanish Language Professional Theatre on the Texas Stage* (New York: Lang, 1990); Nicolas Kanellos (ed.), *Hispanic Theatre in the United States* (Houston: Arte Publico Press, 1984); Jacinto Quirarte (ed.), *Chicano Art History: A Book of Selected Readings* (San Antonio: University of Texas at San Antonio, Research Center for the Arts and Humanities, 1984).
3. For the period from 1965, see Shifra Goldman and Tomas Ybarra Frausto, *Arte Chicano: A Comprehensive Annotated Bibliography of Chicano Art, 1965–1981* (Berkeley: University of California, Chicano Studies Library Publications Unit, 1985).
4. See entries "Chicano Art Networks," vol. 2, pp. 62 and 71; "Chicano Mural Movement," vol. 2, pp. 72–73; "Conferencia Plastica Chicana," vol. 2, p. 266; and "Mujeres Artisticas del Suroeste," vol. 4, p. 828, in *New Handbook of Texas* (Austin: Texas State Historical Association, 1996).
5. Interview with Centro Cultural Aztlan (San Antonio).
6. Interview with Centro Cultural de las Americas (Tucson).
7. Articles of Incorporation, National Association for Latino Art and Culture.
8. Ibid.

9. *Crossing Borders, Cruzando Fronteras: Los Siquiente 500 Años, The Next 500 Years* (San Antonio: NALAC, 1994.)

10. See entry "Mexic-Arte Museum," in *New Handbook of Texas.* (Austin: Texas State Historical Association, 1996).

11. The interviews I conducted follow: Xicanindio (Mesa, Arizona), Dina Lopez-Woodwards, July 28, 1995; Movimiento Artistico del Rio Salado (MARS, Phoenix), Ralph Cordoba, July 28, 1995; Borderlands Theatre (Tucson); Adriana Valenzuela, Annabelle Nunez, and Guadalupe Castillo, July 26, 1995; Centro Cultural de Las Americas (Tucson): John Huerta, July 27, 1995; La Peña Cultural Center (Berkeley); Fernando Torres, July 22, 1995; National Latino Communications Center (Los Angeles), Jose Luis Ruiz, June 20, 1995; Marisa Leal, June 20, 1995, Latino Museum of Art, History, and Culture (Los Angeles), Denise Lugo, July 21, 1995; Jesee Camberos, July 21, 1995; Dr. Antonio Ríos-Bustamante, July 26, 1995; Plaza de la Raza (Los Angeles), Rose Cano, June 20, 1995; Self-Help Graphics (Los Angeles), Sister Karen Bocallero and Tomas Benitez, June 20, 1995; La Raza Galeria Posada (Sacramento), Luis Cabolla, June 18, 1995; Centro Cultural de la Raza (San Diego), Larry Baza, June 21, 1995; Cine Accion (San Francisco), Julia Jaurigi, June 19, 1995; Galeria de la Raza (San Francisco), Amalia Baines and Richard Baines, July 22, 1995; Mexican Museum (San Francisco), Maria Acosta Colon, July 19, 1995; Mission Cultural Center (San Francisco), Maria Martinez, July 21, 1995; Teatro de la Esperanza (San Francisco), Rodrigo Duarte Clark, July 22, 1995; and Teatro Campesino (San Juan Bautista), Phillip Esparza, July 20, 1995; Chicano Humanities and Art Council (Denver), Maruca Salazar, Suzzane Vega, and Carmen Ramirez Epstein, June 15, 1995; Su Teatro (Denver), Anthony Garcia, June 15, 1995; Arte Publico Press (Houston), Dr. Nicolas Kanellos, July 14, 1995; Festival Chicano (Houston), Daniel Bustamante, July 14, 1995; Multicultural Education Through the Arts (Houston), Alice Valdes, July 13, 1995; Teatro Bilingue (Houston), Richard Reyes, July 14, 1995; Centro Cultural Aztlan (San Antonio), Marlena Gonzalez and Ramon Sanchez y Sanchez, September 6, 1995; Guadalupe Cultural Arts Center (San Antonio), Pedro Rodriguez, August 28, 1995; and David Mercado Gonzalez, August 28, 1995.

12. Historical "First Voice" Survey and Current Asessment Completed, *NALAC* newsletter 4, no, 1 (Spring 1996).

13. Interview with Arte Publico Press (Houston)

14. Interview with Xicanindio (Mesa, Arizona).

15. Interview with Centro Cultural de las Americas (Tucson).

16. Interview with Guadalupe Cultural Arts Center (San Antonio).

17. Interview with Festival Chicano (Houston).

18. Interview with Centro Cultural Aztlan (San Antonio).

19. Interview with Guadalupe Cultural Arts Center (San Antonio).

20. Interview with Galeria de la Raza (San Francisco).

21. Interview with Mission Cultural Center (San Francisco).

22. Interview with Chicano Humanities and Arts Council (Denver).

23. Interview with Teatro Bilingue (Houston).
24. Interview with Festival Chicano (Houston).
25. Interview with Centro Cultural de la Raza (San Diego).
26. Ibid.
27. Interview with Multicultural Education and Counseling Through the Arts (Houston).
28. *Willful Neglect: The Smithsonian Institution and U.S. Latinos,* Report of the Smithsonian Institution Task Force on Latino Issues (Washington DC: National Council of La Raza, 1994); Antonio Ríos-Bustamante, *Latinos and Native Americans in Museums: Report of the National Survey and Directory of Historical and Art Museum Professional Personnel* (Tucson: University of Arizona, Mexican American Studies and Research Center, 1997).
29. Interview with Guadalupe Cultural Arts Center (San Antonio).
30. Interview with Festival Chicano (Houston).
31. Interview with National Latino Communications Center (Los Angeles).
32. Interview with Festival Chicano (Houston).
33. Cynthia E. Orozco, "CAB Had it Right the First Time," *San Antonio Express-News,* August 29, 1994.
34. Interview with Borderlands Theatre (Tucson).
35. Interview with Centro Cultural Aztlan (San Antonio).
36. Interview with Teatro Bilingue (Houston).
37. Interview with Centro Cultural Aztlan (San Antonio).
38. Interview with Arte Publico Press (Houston).
39. Ibid.
40. Interview with La Raza Galeria Posada (Sacramento).
41. Ibid.
42. Interview with Centro Cultural Aztlan (San Antonio).

7   PUBLIC HISTORY AND PERFORMANCE: *L.A. REAL*

Theresa Chavez

Performance artist Theresa Chavez examines the importance of perform-
ance for interpreting history. The play L.A. Real *is a dramatic examina-*
tion of the evolution of historical identities of Californiana Mexican mes-
tiza women in southern California over three centuries. Drawing upon
her own experience as a descendant of the historic Californio Lugo family,
Chavez examines the development of, and the massive nineteenth-and
twentieth-century decontextualization of, the history of the native Cali-
forniana Mexican women and resulting distortion of their identity. This
includes real estate boosterism's invention of mythical "Spanish grandee"
and "romantic Mediterranean" identities, which obscured and denied the
real Indian and Mexican historical presence. Chavez recontextualizes a
history and culture that have been literally paved over in order to build
the housing tracts, parking lots, and freeways of the Trans-Pacific mega-
lopolis of the twenty-first century.

—The editors

The story . . . the teller . . . the truth . . . the details . . . the rumors . . . the
opinions . . . the basic lies . . . the angle . . . the light . . . the version . . . the
distance from the event . . . the tale of one city . . . the romance . . . the leg-
ends . . . the sequel . . . the saga . . . the reporter . . . the portrait . . . the
transcription . . . the frame . . . the family name . . . the family lie . . . the
translation . . . the remembering . . . the story . . . the storyteller . . .

—*L.A. Real*
Slides that play in a loop as audience enters theater

FIRST PERFORMANCE

In third grade I came home from school with a book titled *The History
of Monterey Park*. Upon showing it to my mother, she declared that the
sullen-looking gentleman pictured opposite the title page was my rela-

tive. She knew his name but was not quite sure of the exact lineage—some great, great, great, great grandfather of mine.

In 1810 Don Antonio Maria Lugo received a permit from the Spanish government to graze cattle on 29,000 acres. Later referred to as a land grant, it encompassed a number of Los Angeles-area cities, including what is now the working-class suburb of Monterey Park. The complete meaning of that knowledge was beyond my grasp then, but the moment of receiving that information was an exciting one. My mother's pride shone through as she, for the first time in my short life, explained the "story" of our family. The story, as I was later to discover, was an oral history full of misinformation and nostalgia for a culture that barely exists today.

I returned to my third-grade classroom and explained to the teacher my unbelievable news. I was related to one of the founding families of Los Angeles. His picture was in our third-grade reader. She, too, was amazed and asked if I would make a presentation to all the third-grade classes. I agreed, and soon after, in a blue velvet dress that my mother had sewn for the occasion, I delivered a short explanation of a history as told by my mother. My first public performance of my family's history was a success. The students and teachers were impressed and listened attentively. I remember holding notes in case I forgot an important detail. I can still see my writing on those yellow and green index cards—soldier, rancho, king of Spain, cattle, adobe, taxes. Through the act of public presentation I had personally accepted the weight of my own history.

From that day forward, I knew that the story would have to be told and retold. I had no idea what form those stories would take, but I embraced the familial responsibility of being the keeper and caretaker of our past.

It was my mother who told me many of the stories of our family. The oral culture of the Californios has always been based in the family. She was repeating what she had been told or what she seemed to remember. But there was always some self-doubt. She used phrases like, "You know, that's what they used to say." As if she was acknowledging the half-truth she was passing down to me. She was born in 1921 into a family of nine. It was her father's side that bore the Lugo line. She was raised in the era of the Hollywood version of Old California—rich, fiesta making Spaniards, always dressed for a party, lace on the women, bolero vests on the men, dancing the night and day away. She was born into that myth. There was almost nothing left of that past, so why not begin to make it up. A little history here, a little Hollywood there. She always said that Don Antonio Maria Lugo received his land grant because he was "a very brave soldier and the King of Spain rewarded him with this great rancho." Of course, Antonio Lugo probably never met the King of Spain, but the majesty of such a statement made everyone feel . . . real good. Spanish connections. Royal connections. The dominion. Maybe we're all Spanish to this day. Pure bloods. Lighter, better, more European. She believes this, despite the fact that the Lugos came from what is now Northern Mexico—Sonora—and had lived there for possibly two or three generations. And, at the point that my family came to L.A. in 1771, Spanish citizens had been in this part of the world for over two hundred and fifty years. But she was never told this and never learned otherwise. I'm sure that if anything had truly been passed down through six generations, it was these stories about "Spanish" ancestors and the "attitude" that goes with them.

—Raquel, Mestiza Narrator
L.A. Real

FIRST BRIDGE

The exploration and articulation of the self is not the exclusive territory of art, but it remains one of the prime forces behind the artist's instinct to create. In contemporary theater forms, most notably in performance, the practice of using personal history has become a rite of passage for the writer-performer. Many begin here. Some move on to other passions; others continue to mine their own lives as a means of self-expression. This is not where I began, but as I matured as a theater artist, it was definitely a bridge that was necessary to cross.

Twenty-five years after my third-grade performance, I began the process of uncovering a history buried under the weight of movie nostalgia, historical romanticism, and a real estate industry hell-bent on profiting from an architecture that inflated a mission past that no longer existed. Having crossed over, I realize that it is not so much the bridge but rather an actual place that I will have to return to throughout my lifetime, especially because my own past touches on a public history that illuminates the sociopolitical, ethnic, cultural, economic, and geographic life of Los Angeles and the Southwest.

I could just as easily pretend that none of this happened. That I am not related to this past. But, I still find traces of it in my body. They sit alongside the mercury and fluorocarbons I can trace as well. It would be easy to forget amidst the strangle of freeway around my neck. Forget the complicated past that covers seven generations, three federal governments, a land grant that would now cover six different cities, the breaking of the 1848 Treaty of Guadalupe Hidalgo, a barter economy turned cash economy, a crooked Land Commission, real estate promotions, and the attempt to undo the use of all indigenous languages. I could go about my business and forget. But I see pictures. I hear stories. I read the printed word. A tribe of my people lived here. But whatever it is they created, it no longer exists. Their songs do not get sung. Their land has been cemented over. Their paths have become our boulevards. I can barely see the world that was theirs. Why should I remember a past that only complicates my living, my understanding of who I am? I could simply selectively edit my own history. Give my own face a new meaning. Be an American mongrel. Or define myself according to any given historical moment—Californiana, Mexicana, Mexican-American, Chicana, Hispanic, Latina, Mestiza . . .

—Raquel, Mestiza Narrator
L.A. Real

FIRST MEMORY

Many artists have used the performance form to uncover the past and present alternative histories. This politicized form has given a number of writers and writer-performers permission to challenge traditional assumptions about history, cultural identity, and gender.[1] In the works of May Sun, Joan Hotchkis, Dan Kwong, and others, theater, photography, sculpture, music, anthropology, historical research, and personal archeology provide the media for a wealth of images, sounds, textures, and ideas. In Sun's collaborative performance work, *L.A./River/China/Town,* she invites viewers to walk into history. The audience crosses a river of sand and enters a settlement like those that housed Chinese immigrant railroad workers along the L.A. River in the 1870s. The four white pitched tents contain a series of tableaux unfolding the hidden myth and history of Old Chinatown, including the L.A. Chinatown Massacre of 1871 and ultimately Sun's own nightmare vision of the L.A. River overflowing with animals and ghosts.[2]

L.A. Real is an interdisciplinary performance theater piece that I wrote, produced, and directed.[3] A hybrid between traditional theater and performance art, it utilizes historical and contemporary characters written in Brechtian fashion, as well as utilizing traditional theater dialogic forms. The theater piece also incorporates painting, photography, and video, used to imagistically represent a lost L.A. The characters include a contemporary mestiza narrator who searches for her family's past, two mid-nineteenth-century Californio rancheros, a contemporary Gabrielino narrator who is a part-time convenience-store clerk and part-time actor, and a contemporary real estate agent who traffics in Mission and Spanish Revival homes (the latter character developed in collaboration with cultural critic Norman Klein). *L.A. Real* also exists as a one-person version in which the Mestiza Narrator is the sole character and storyteller. The Californios represent the actual history, while the other characters represent how history is remembered, distorted, used, rediscovered, lost, and reclaimed. The rancheros' story of losing their land to the onslaught of America's Manifest Destiny is told through vignettes in linear form. The other characters move in and around this loose narrative to rebuild or—in the case of the real estate agent—erase memory. (See Figure 7.1.)

> . . . but there's this history from hundreds of years ago and then there's me, now, with a big gap in between. A gap filled with my ancestors caught in a place where going forward meant loss or frustration and going backward meant searching through the rubble of human cinder and broken bone. I work here part-time and I'm a part-time actor—film and television. Usually playing Plains Indians—you know, Cherokee, Lakota. Of course this doesn't help to straighten out my reality. But it is beginning to drive me to try to make a connection with my mysterious past and my amorphous present.
>
> —Joe, Gabrielino Narrator
> *L.A. Real*

FIRST CRITIQUE

From 1991 to 1993, *L.A. Real* was presented on various stages and in numerous venues in southern California and New York. The piece was very well received by both audiences and critics. Audiences were struck by a history they had little knowledge of and touched by the characters' personal journeys. Latino audiences were especially grateful for the work. Many were also introduced to, and found they were able to enjoy and learn from, a new theater format. The interrelated use of text, music, and image to relay a dense and unfamiliar history proved successful because the audience was guided by characters that genuinely expressed their need to uncover the past. For some, though, the real estate agent character was a difficult pill to swallow. In his attempts to erase the past in order to sell homes, offices, and eventually Olvera Street, he cut too close to the bone. The representation of the actual history made some audience members and critics uncomfortable. They felt he was a bit too accusatory.

> Wouldn't you like to have a plantation of your own? Five hundred Indian peasants working in the front yard? An old Franciscan mission up the road, near an Indian cemetery filled with unmarked graves?
> Well, with our Mission Revival special those memories are not lost! You're inside a lathe-and-plaster, five bedroom, Spanish stucco house, almost three

Figure 7.1. Actress Rose Portillo, *L.A. Real* dramatic performance. *Photo courtesy of Craig Schwartz Photography.*

thousand square feet, on a double city lot. Such attention to detail. Simulated adobe arches. Simulated rafters. A little moorish dome near the upstairs bathroom. A fireplace big enough to roast a small pig, or at least some marinated chicken breast, with your own home-made salsa. By the patio stands an army of Indian peasants, done for us by the Franklin Mint, fully detailed, even down to their torn clothing. Each Indian is stooped over, three inches high, with a corn milagro in one hand.

Think of all those lazy afternoons around the barbeque with your friends. "Tell us about the history of the Missions." You'll just smile . . . "What system of crop rotation do you favor? How would you discipline an Indian who refused to take Christ as his saviour?" And over there, they'll see your life-size statue of Father Francisco. Three hundred pounds of molded lead, painted so life-like, they'll feel tempted to convert! Big, isn't he! This is a collectible that will reward you in years to come, and give you pleasure along the way.

Whatever the trials of everyday life—carjacking, rising healthcare costs, the reduced buying power for the middle class—these hardy little Indians will keep toiling ceaselessly, gathering your imaginary monthly harvest. A monument to racial harmony in your own backyard, even after the percentage of Anglos in L.A. County drops to practically nothing.

Of course, the Mission Revival houses were built to last, during the twenties, when there were more white Protestants here than in any other city in America. In those days, mission facades were built to remind Americans of how white management won the west. Now all the remnants of mission landscape are gone. Even the San Fernando Mountains are gone most of the year. But not here, not on your patio. In your Mission Revival backyard, the fiesta goes on.

Need something to microwave for your fiesta? Something picante? You're only minutes from lovely downtown Encino, on freeways built over the original Mission road. Who's that near the underpass? An illegal alien walks beside the road. The dusty Santa Anas are blowing, but you zoom ahead, leaving him standing alone by the parched roadway like so many other Mexicans in centuries gone by. You are part of a tradition. And the tradition is part of you.

—Dick Richman, Real Estate Agent
L.A. Real

Sylvie Drake, former theater critic for the *Los Angeles Times*, had great praise for the solo version of *L.A. Real*, which she saw performed at the National Women's Theatre Festival in July 1992. Her review said the production was "laced with a kind of pragmatic irony that never takes itself too seriously, full of rancor for the savaging of the land, imbued with the richness of the past, poetic but never so lyrical as to be out of step with present reality."[4] But her subsequent review of the five-person version changed its tone. She especially had problems with the real estate agent. She stated, "The words of [the] Gabrielino Indian and the fast-talking real estate salesman feel like pronouncements chiefly designed to be politically correct."[5]

I was surprised by Drake's criticism and found her use of the term "politically correct" to be, as I stated in an op-ed article published in the *Los Angeles Times*, "reactionary shorthand."[6] I thought the meaning of the phrase was obscured, since she did not further describe or clarify her statement. I further stated in response to her review, "Even in the case where one speaks from the experience of one's own group, the review implies one can be acting in a 'politically correct' manner. According to this review, even if one is speaking from historically documented material, there is still the possibility that one may be speaking too clearly, too offensively." Her response did leave me wondering if it is possible to dramatically depict a history rife with ethnic strife without showing the racism.

FIRST CLAIM

From the third-grade moment to this thirty-something moment, I have been staking a claim on the part of myself that is attached to this place—Los Angeles. I have been seeking a memory that is still unfulfilled. I have hoped that, in doing so, I will touch a chord in those who wish to hear the land and its past inhabitants speak. The simple act of voicing an unheard story is powerful. The subsequent act of hearing it can simply be instructive, but it can also be physically and spiritually moving. This is especially so in the ritual space of the theater. The performer and the performance surround the audience, altering their perceptions of a past they thought they were familiar with. In *L.A. Real* the characters not only represent a history but are actively battling with the notion of who owns that history and who has the right to tell its stories. They are engaged with history in a dance that affects them personally and politically. Researching the history and developing *L.A. Real* into a performance piece has clarified my identity and my relationship to the political history of Los Angeles. But I have come to realize that it is an endless process. As I continue the search, there will be other discoveries and other performances.

I am looking for the actual woman who was here, my great grandmother, and her mother too. The mestizas. These women who built this pueblo, who began their days at 4 a.m., who bore far too many children, who buried their husbands twice their age. Maybe that's when they found their peace. When their children were grown and their husbands were gone but they were still only in their mid-thirties. Their brothers and their husbands were usually called españoles. It was more important that the men be thought of as sangre puros. They worshipped pure blood, thinking it kept them closer to Jesus Cristo. The culture could excuse the tainted bloodline in their women. If the men could just remember to stay in character—los hombres de razon—civilized Spanish men of reason. But she could live closer to the truth. I am looking for her. She now rides like a phantom over this city looking for herself, looking for a place to touch down. The landscape is recognizable, but there is no communication with the control tower. She needs permission to land, but they cannot give her clearance. They treat her like a foreigner, a UFO, they do not recognize her. She radios them that she knows the earth that lies beneath this tangle of cement surfaces. She spots the rancho, the path to the center of the old pueblo, el rio de los temblores. She knows she once lived here, before any of this. But without clearance, she may crash, she may disintegrate . . . again. She is part of that forgotten moment. A moment transformed in the hands of the new Americans. Erased and redrawn to satisfy the blank imaginations of those who came here to acquire their part of her. Remade in their own likeness with their own short memory. They replaced empty, vacant mission ghost towns with curio shops for the Midwestern mind. And it may seem that this is what has been left for me. But if I reach back to trace myself I feel something, I know something in my heart. I can't specify it. My genetic lines are criss-crossed. I start to go back and leaps and bounds happen. The only thing I know for a fact is that it all happened right here in this city. I want to make a place for you to touch down. Do not look for carretas or clipper ships patrolling the coastline like before. Follow the freeway. Please make an appearance. I'm calling for you. I'll wait for you to come.

—Raquel, Mestiza Narrator
L.A. Real

ENDNOTES

1. Michael Vanden Heuvel in his book *Performing Drama/Dramatizing Performance: Alternative Theater and the Dramatic Text* (Ann Arbor: University of Michigan Press, 1993) states

   provocative alternatives have been investigated within theater's margins, and exciting new fields of dramatic and performative inquiry have opened up. Such work has grown beyond early attempts at sentimentalizing ritual and venerating performance as the panacea for, or affirmative response to, postmodern consciousness. The new performance drama is grounded more substantially in history, its artists increasingly aware that the past has a hold on the present. Rather than trying to escape history by retrodicting the past or by hypostatizing the present, contemporary theater addresses the past by scrutinizing the role that theater plays in the making of the history, whether it be through investigation of past canonical tests by The Wooster Group, of archetypal and cultural myths by Robert Wilson, or of individual consciousness by Samuel Beckett and Sam Shephard, In each case, the artist involved has determined that the fundamental space between text and performance provides a rich source of creative energy which can be used to create deconstructive dramaturgies for exploring cultura and personal history. In doing so, these quantum artists have both expanded theater's range of articulation and returned it to its social and cultural matrix.

2. Linda Frye Burnham, "Alternative Histories: Artists Challenge the Official Story," *High Performance,* Winter 1992.

3. *L.A. Real,* Theresa Chavez, c. 1993, 1992.

4. Sylvie Drake, "Women Continue Empowerment Theme," *Los Angeles Times,* August 1, 1992.

5. Sylvie Drake, "A Bigger 'L.A. Real' Changes Its Tone," *Los Angeles Times,* April 3, 1994.

6. Theresa Chavez, " 'L.A. Real': Personal Work Not Meant to be Offensive," *Los Angeles Times,* April 26, 1993.

8 MÁS PRODUCTION OF ART FOR THE MASSES: SERIGRAPHS OF SELF-HELP GRAPHIC ARTS, INC.

Reina Alejandra Prado Saldivar

Art historian Reina Alejandra Prado Saldivar poses the question of how a community art center takes agency in defining itself, its role, and its production through a specific program. Examined here is the experience of East Los Angeles Self-Help Graphic Arts (SHGA), a community applied-arts program.

By presenting a historical narrative of the Ateliérs that began in 1983, Prado shows that these biannual art workshops propelled SHGA into becoming a clearinghouse for Chicano art and artists. A second concern is Self-Help Graphics' commitment to empowering the Mexican American community of East Los Angeles through artistic endeavors, as carried out in the Ateliérs. Further discussed is how SHGA exhibited, distributed, and packaged the serigraphs produced at these Ateliérs.

—*The editors*

At the 1996 National Association of Chicana and Chicano Studies conference held in Chicago, I had the opportunity with fellow colleagues to present a paper on the role of art institutions, and how they present and represent the Chicano/Latino community through exhibits and policies.[1] A question I raised is "How does a community art center take agency in defining itself, its role, and the production through a specific program?" An example of an institution taking agency in its representation is the biannual Ateliérs held at Self-Help Graphic Arts, Inc. (SHGA), a community-based art institution located in East Los Angeles. The Ateliérs are workshops that experiment in the media of silkscreen and monoprint. By presenting a historical narrative on the Ateliérs, which began in 1983, I propose to show that these biannual workshops propelled SHGA into becoming a clearinghouse for Chicano art and its artists. My second concern regards Self-Help Graphics' commitment to empowering the Mexican American community of East Los Angeles through artistic endeavors, as carried out in the Ateliérs. My third concern is how SHGA exhibited, distributed, and packaged the serigraphs produced at these Ateliérs.

Sister Karen Boccalero, with the help of two Mexican national artists, Antonio Ibañez and Carlos Bueno, opened Self-Help Graphics in 1968 from her garage. Four years later Self-Help's charter was established, and Sister Karen found a larger space, which now is the home of the center.[2] By 1974 Self-Help had implemented programs that reflected some of its objectives and an approach to art education with an emphasis on culture, aesthetics, and skills. These programs include a commercial and artistic graphics and silkscreen workshop; the Galería Otra Vez Art exhibition space; the Barrio Mobil Art Studio, a program that provided art activities and technical assistance in the areas of silkscreen, printing, photography, sculpture, and puppetry to a minimum of 9,000 participants, a majority of whom were youngsters in the East Los Angeles area;[3] and the annual Day of the Dead show. These programs were designed to provide a means by which artists could become more effective in the community. Thus, Self-Help's connection of cultural production with the community had resonances with the function of Chicano art as articulated in the 1970s.

Founding member Sister Karen Boccalero, a Franciscan nun, had received artistic training in printmaking. She believed in empowering the Chicano community she lived in by instilling pride in culture through art. In 1975 Self-Help began a training program for artists in the graphic medium. One of these programs was the Mexican American Master Printers program, which helped set the precedent for the first Ateliérs. The Master Printers program was intended to be a two-year course to train artists in various print-making techniques, such as woodcut, linocut, serigraphy, photo silkscreen, and intaglio, thereby qualifying them to compete for employment in commercial and advertising agencies. Scholarships were available to students on the basis of need, and financial aid was distributed in three forms: free instruction, free supplies, and monetary scholarship. A preference was shown to applicants of Mexican American descent because of Self-Help's cultural agenda; however, the program was not restricted to this ethnic group. Recruitment for the program was done through art centers in the Los Angeles area, community centers, churches, and schools. Opportunities for artists to exhibit their works in a gallery setting were also granted.

Nevertheless, there has been some criticism of Self-Help Graphics' approach to the community and the arts, primarily from Shifra Goldman, a noted art historian. She has stated that because Self-Help's stance is not explicitly a "political one," as an art institution it could "skirt the more troublesome and controversial politics of the Chicano movement and

Chicano art addressed to these issues." However, I believe the case is quite the contrary, thanks to Self-Help Graphics's mission of working within the Mexican American community of East Los Angeles. Self-Help became a space for Chicano artists to freely create art that addressed issues affecting the Chicano community, as well as those that impinged upon personal politics. Thus, Self-Help's connection of cultural production with the community has resonance with the goals of Chicano art as articulated in the 1970s. As Rudolfo Anaya has stated, "Artists along with philosophers were articulating the new language and visual imagery to match the times."[4] The Chicano artist became the interpreter of signs and themes that were emerging during the height of the Chicano movement.

Because of SHGA's strong commitment to the Mexican American community of East Los Angeles, it has a pool of talented and eager Chicano/a artists from which to recruit for the various programs. An example of this is Gronk, a member of the Chicano art collective ASCO, who exhibited and worked frequently at SHGA. As a favor to Sister Karen, Gronk agreed to do a series of prints in 1982 known as the Special Project.[5] The only documentation of this project is in a pamphlet produced in 1988 that discusses the history of the Ateliér program,[6] which could be due to a falling out Gronk and Sister Karen had after the Special Project was completed.

Gronk's involvement in the Special Project needs to be addressed because as a Chicano artist, he was able to bridge the relationship between art and market.[7] I believe Sister Karen made a conscious choice of recruiting Gronk for the Special Project because of his artistic talent and because his art was marketable the strongly emerging middle-class Hispanic community of Los Angeles. Further, by having Gronk as the first artist of the Ateliérs, Self-Help was setting the tone for who would be invited to participate in the Ateliérs: artists who produced high-quality work and were able to sell in both the "ethnic" and Anglo art-buying market. Despite the situation that developed between Sister Karen and Gronk, she continued the Ateliérs. She tapped into the artist roster that she had been compiling to obtain artists for the first Ateliér.

ATELIÉR PROGRAM
HISTORY AND EXHIBITIONS

An overall history of the Ateliérs can be found in the SHGA archives housed at the California Ethnic and Multicultural Archive at the University of California, Santa Barbara. One of the original documents, which was mailed to artists in 1983, called upon artists to outline the structure and goals of the first annual Experimental Screenprint Ateliér and Exhibition.

> Drawing on over ten years of community arts experience, this Ateliér was organized by Self-Help Graphics with the intention of giving a select group of artists of extremely varied backgrounds, styles, and aesthetics an opportunity to work together in a format largely determined by the artist themselves, with the objectives of giving all of the participants the maximum degree of freedom possible in individually and collectively exploring and manipulating the screenprint medium in the process of conceiving and of executing their respective pieces. It was not intended, therefore, as a simple introduction to screenprinting, but rather as a genuine atelier, or workshop, with serious, finished works as its goal.[8]

What makes the Ateliérs unique is that Self-Help provided artists who would normally not have had the economic means to produce a limited edition serigraph, to hire a master printer, and to have space to create art. Furthermore, those who participated in the Ateliérs had the opportunity to work in a professional setting and collaborate with other artists while also adding to their portfolios. In exchange, the group of artists participating received a complete series of the prints and their proofs while Self-Help Graphics kept the balance of each edition for documentation, archives, and sales.

Each cycle of the Ateliér has an exhibit at the Galería Otra Vez, providing an opportunity for the community to appreciate and view works by Chicano artists. The program also addressed the role of the art market. Due to the accessibility in price of these silkscreens, Self-Help is fostering an art-buying public interested in Chicano art. For example, from the first Ateliér the complete series was available at $100, or $15 per individual copy, a situation that has changed.[9]

Alex Alferov, curator of The Exhibition Print Program, displayed ten to fifty prints in various public and private venues throughout the greater Los Angeles area, as well as in the Galería Otra Vez. Through this program the art of up-and-coming Chicano and Chicana artists gained exposure nationally, and their art was appreciated outside the East Los Angeles community, which served as wonderful examples of the diversity and talent seen in Chicano art.[10]

Other projects ensued that allowed Self-Help Graphics and the Ateliérs to become part of international and national programs. One of these projects worth noting is the 1987 collaboration of Self-Help with El Colegío de la Frontera Norte and Gil Cardenas of the Galería Sin Fronteras in Austin, Texas. A binational atelier was held in which prints published by both Mexican and Chicano artists illustrated the theme of "Carnalismo: Cuates, Compadres y Hermanos" (Friendship in the Life Cycle:

Brotherhood and Sisterhood), during the Fourth International Festival de la Raza in Tijuana, Mexico.[11] One of the participating artists was Patssi Valdez, whose serigraph entitled *LA/TJ* describes the ironic cultural exchange between Los Angeles and Tijuana. On Broadway, a main street in downtown Los Angeles, there are many Latinos walking the streets, while in Tijuana, there are many Anglo-Americans walking the main thoroughfare of Revolución.

The 1988–89 Ateliér was a national screenprint workshop organized for the "Chicano Art: Resistance and Affirmation" traveling exhibit. The national atelier consisted of invited Chicano artists who represented nine regions of the United States. The artists produced limited silkscreen editions of original works. As the first major outreach program of this exhibition, the national atelier, through high artistic quality and varied visual content, was expected to raise national and international public awareness of the Ateliér program, Chicano artists, and Chicano art in general.[12]

Two subsequent exhibits featured the serigraphs generated during the biannual Ateliérs and brought attention to the role of Self-Help Graphics as an art institution that consistently produces contemporary Chicano art. The shows "Chicano Expressions" (1994) and "Across the Street: Self-Help Graphics and Chicano Art in Los Angeles" (1995) exemplify the recent response to representations of the sphere of Chicano art. "Chicano Expressions," which exhibited thirty prints from the Ateliérs, was seen in Johannesburg, South Africa, and in Europe. Funding was provided by the Arts America Program of the United States Information Agency, and the exhibit was curated by SHGA.[13] "Across the Street" was curated by the Laguna Art Museum in conjunction with Self-Help under the premise of acquiring 170 prints produced during the print workshops.[14] Questions of who has agency in defining Chicano art and the role of the art market came into play in these two traveling exhibits. How does SHGA retain its autonomy when state and federal agencies provide funding for museums to purchase and package Chicano art as an American art form? What does it mean to have a division of the United States government package and promote Chicano art as part of American culture, given the sociohistorical relationship between Mexicans or Chicanos and Anglo-Americans?

SELF-HELP GRAPHICS ATELIÉRS: PRODUCTION OF CHICANO ART

Artists working during the 1980s produced images that reified the ideals of the early days of the Chicano art movement, which affirmed pride in culture and political activism, yet reflected the evolving styles of contemporary Chicano art. Many of the artists applied indigenous imagery along with contemporary urban symbols, as well as strong cultural icons from both Mexican and American cultures (see Figures 8.1, 8.2, and 8.3). Yreina Cervántez, for example, included the ocelot and contemporary historical scenes in many of her works. *Danza Ocelot*, a color serigraph from Ateliér II (1983), is a portrait of the artist wearing a mask. Cervántez used imagery of Mesoamerican indigenous cultures, as well as Catholic and Chicana symbols, as if the syncretism of culture were something inherently Chicano. The selection of the ocelot (Nahuatl for jaguar) can perhaps be understood as making reference to her Aztec ancestry. And the placement of symbols on the four axes of her face—on the north an eye; on the east the sacred heart; on the south the crescent moon; and on the west a skull—refers to the Aztec cosmology. The Chicana imagery encompasses all these elements, as well as many of those that reflect a contemporary symbology, such as the black bracelet that alludes to the women of the barrio, the *chola* and the *tira*, pointing out that she is a Chicana/indigenous princess.

Another example that combines familiar icons with urban imagery while employing humor through a play on words and recognizable cultural icons is Alfredo de Batuc's *Seven Views of City Hall* (Ateliér IX, 1987). In this piece the artist refers to both the name of the city of Los Angeles, as in *La Reina de Los Angeles* (Our Queen of Angels) and that of the Virgin of Guadalupe. He replaces the image of the Virgin with that of Los Angeles City Hall and retains the icons of the crescent moon and the archangel with various animals, thus injecting the image of Los Angeles City Hall into the format of colonial paintings of the Virgin de Guadalupe. Along the same line of using Catholic and in a sense feminine iconography is Patssi Valdez's *The Dressing Table* (Ateliér XII, 1988). Valdez addresses the tradition of women maintaining their private space through the use of altars.

Another theme depicted by participating artists in the Ateliérs is that of United States imperialism prevalent in both Latin America and the United States upon the Chicano/Latino community. One example is the serigraph by Alex Donis, *Rio por no llorar/I laugh so not to cry* (Ateliér XII, 1988). He makes reference to Carmen Miranda, the Brazilian Hollywood movie star of the 1940s, as read in the title piece of the Ateliér. The woman in bondage embodies Latin Americans as female and something to be objectified and owned. Natural resources and products from Latin America are seen in her headdress, as well in the barb wire, making this a very political piece with a stark contrast to the artistic presentation. Border issues are another theme prevalent in many works done by Chicano artists. Malaquias Montoya's *Si se puede/Yes it can be done* (Ateliér

Figure 8.1. Artist Patssi Valdez and printer Balboa in the silk screen studio East Lost Angeles Self-Help Graphics. *Photo Courtesy Self-Help Graphics.*

Figure 8.2. Experimental screenprint Atelier V, Yreina Cervántez, Alonzo Davis, artists. *Photo courtesy of Self-Help Graphics.*

Dia de Los Muertos
Day of the Dead 10th Anniversary

November 7 1982. Self Help Graphics, Los Angeles, CA
Partially Funded by N.E.A.

Figure 8.3. Day of the Dead 10th Anniversary—November 2, 1982, Gronk, artist. *Photo courtesy of Self-Help Graphics.*

XIII, 1989) expresses the idea that Mexican Americans are as indigenous to this land as the aloe vera plant, seen in the serigraph. Montoya employs nationalist icons of both the United States and Mexico to describe the U.S.-Mexico border as one of political boundaries that many must cut across through barb wire fence.

Through the biannual Ateliérs, up-and-coming artists have been given the opportunity to create art that is reflective of the diverse nature seen in Chicano life. One artist of recent note is Yolanda Gonzalez, who is part of the new generation of Chicano artists and in many ways Self-Help's poster girl. Gonzalez has participated in many of the art programs offered at Self-Help and was given the opportunity to join the 1991 Ateliér. Two of the serigraphs she did are *Vaquero* and *Mi Indio,* which were included in the traveling exhibits "Chicano Expressions" and "Across the Street."

Several artists have participated in more than one Ateliér and have developed a unique and distinct style that is easily recognizable, as in the case of Leo Limon, Diane Gamboa, Margaret Garcia, and Yreina Cervántez. The establishment of the Ateliér program in 1983, which continues to the present day, has contributed to the diversity and richness of the graphic medium while also pushing the boundaries of what Chicano art is. The artists who have participated in the annual Ateliérs are just a sample of artists working within the graphic tradition.

What lies ahead for Self-Help Graphics and the Ateliérs? Up to the present, the Ateliérs have been quite successful, thanks to the caliber of artists invited to participate. Self-Help Graphics continues to uphold its mission of empowering the Mexican American community by providing instruction, holding cultural events like the Day of the Dead celebration, and offering the biannual Ateliérs. With all this recognition and success, however, can Self-Help Graphics retain its unique quality of being the community art center of East Los Angeles? Has Self-Help Graphics lost its connection to the East Los Angeles community in order to expand the Chicano art-buying market, thereby catering to other, non-Chicano communities? More extensive analysis of the full scope of Self-Help Graphics is needed, as this essay has looked at only one of programs at Self-Help Graphic Arts, whose programs have opened the doors of opportunity for Chicano artists and are introducing another aspect of Chicano art to the art world.[15]

ENDNOTES

1. This paper (chapter) was presented at the 1996 National Association for Chicana and Chicano Studies (NACCS) conference in Chicago. I was part

of a panel comprising graduate students from the University of Arizona (E. Liane Hernandez) and the City University of New York (Rocío Aranda-Alvarado), with Dr. Raquel Rubio-Goldsmith as chair of the panel and Dr. Antonia Castañeda as respondent. We all presented papers on "La Belleza: Reclaiming Spaces, Constructing Identities from Coast to Coast."

2. The original date of Self-Help Graphic Arts (SHGA) varies from 1969, 1972, or 1973, depending on what publication is read. I selected the date of 1969 because this is when it began in Sister Karen's garage. The dates of 1972 and 1973 relate to their new home on Gage and Cesar Chavez and the year their charter was in place.

3. Community Arts Program in Los Angeles, Draft 77 written by Roger W. Gomez, Research Assistant, UCLA School of Architecture and Urban Planning, February 6, 1978 (draft was sent to SHGA, Inc.), CEMA Archives, box 9, folder 18.

4. Rudolfo Anaya, "Aztlan," in Rudolfo Anaya and Francisco Lomeli (eds.), *Aztlan: Essays on the Chicano Homeland* (Albuquerque: University of New Mexico Press, 1989), 230–41.

5. Author interview with Gronk (Glugio Nicandro), March 24–29, 1995.

6. *The Ateliér Program—East Los Angeles* (Los Angeles: Self-Help Graphic Arts, 1988), n.p.

7. Gronk was represented by the Saxon-Lee Gallery while he was also working with ASCO. ASCO was also gaining more notoriety as artist of the avant-garde, particularly because of their work at Los Angeles Contemporary Exhibitions (LACE). See Zanetta Kosiba-Vargas, "Harry Gamboa and ASCO: The Emergence and Development of a Chicano Art Group, 1971–1987," Ph.D. diss., University of Michigan, 1988.

8. Publicity correspondence, 1983–1985, CEMA Archives, box 5, folder 3. A call to artists and announcement of the Ateliér program and accompanying exhibit.

9. Ibid. Margaret Garcia in 1986, with her serigraph entitled *Red Bitch,* received high publicity and placed serigraphs from SHGA at a higher market rate. Unpublished interview with Margaret Garcia, April 1996, Tucson, Arizona.

10. *The Ateliér Program—East Los Angeles* (Los Angeles: Self-Help Graphic Arts, 1988), n.p.

11. "The Ateliér Expands, in ibid., and "Taller de Seragrafia," IV International Festival de la Raza, Tijuana, Mexico, 1987, CEMA Archives, box 9, folder 3, exhibit card.

12. Chicano Art: Resistance & Affirmation (CARA) exhibit at UCLA Wight Gallery, 1988, CEMA Archives, box 8, folder 4, part of abstract found among correspondence to and from SHGA to national Ateliér project coordinator.

13. Foreword in *Chicano Expressions: Serigraphs from the Collection of Self-Help Graphics,* exhibition catalog (Washington, DC: United States Information Agency, 1992), 4.

14. Foreword in *Across the Street: Self-Help Graphics and Chicano Art in Los Angeles,* exhibition catalog (Laguna, CA: Laguna Arts Museum, 1995), 5.

15. I would like to thank Sister Karen Boccalero, Tomás Benitez, the staff and

artists at Self-Help Graphics, as well as Salvador Guereña and his staff at the California Ethnic and Multicultural Archives at the University of California, Santa Barbara, for their time and help with my research on the Ateliérs and Self-Help. This chapter is a working paper to be included in my master's thesis.

9 SUMMARY OF THE 1991–1992 NATIONAL SURVEY OF LATINO AND NATIVE AMERICAN PROFESSIONAL MUSEUM PERSONNEL

Antonio Ríos-Bustamante

In the final chapter, Antonio Ríos-Bustamante discusses the results of a 1992 national survey of Latino and Native American representation among museum professionals. This survey was modeled on a successful survey of Latino librarians, which is credited with stimulating the training and recruitment of Latinos in that field. The survey was sent to 2,000 American historical and art museums based upon lists from the American Association of Museums. A further 400 museums were included because of their location in areas with high Latino and Native populations or because they were Latino or Native American museums. The author concludes with recommendations for further research, recruitment, promotion, and retention of Latino and Native American museum professional staff.

—The editors

In 1991–92 the Mexican American Studies and Research Center, University of Arizona, sponsored the first National Survey of Latino and Native American Professional Museum Personnel.[1] Conducted with the support of the American Association of Museums (AAM) and the American Historical Association's Committee on Minority Historians, the survey was initiated in order to produce a report on the status of Latinos and Native Americans in the profession. A second aspect was the compilation and publication of a directory of Latino and Native American museum professionals as a national reference work for museums and libraries.[2]

METHODOLOGY AND RATIONALE

The survey included states with a Latino and Native American population of at least 10 percent and specific metropolitan areas with major Latino and Native American populations. Native American tribal and

Latino museums were included as a matter of course. The 1,000 largest historical and 1,000 largest art museums comprised the major portion of the survey pool. The survey targeted those institutions with operating budgets of more than $500,000 and museums located in areas of large Latino and Native American representation. Announcements of the survey were made in professional newsletters, such as those of the AAM, the American Association for State and Local History, and the American Historical Association, and resulted in a number of institutions not originally included in the target group contacting the sponsors in order to participate in the survey.

Two versions of the questionnaire were sent out, one for history museums and one for art museums. Except for titles and references to either history or art, the questionnaires were identical. Both had three parts, the first of which included sixteen general questions designed to provide a profile of the status of Latino and Native American professional employment in museums. These questions focused on the Latino and Native American ethnic breakdown of the entire professional staff, as well as a gender breakdown of the Latino and Native American portion thereof. Similar questions focused on the aforementioned breakdowns for administrative and maintenance positions. Other questions addressed the status of affirmative action programs and requirements for the institution. Part II listed forty-one employment titles categorized under the headings Collections/Research Staff, Program Staff, Administrative Staff, and Maintenance Staff. This section asked for total number of employees for each title, the Latino and Native American portion for each title, and the gender breakdown of that portion.

Part III of the questionnaire was designed to provide biographical information to be used in compiling a national directory of Latino and Native American professional personnel in historical and art museums. The directory was modeled in part on the highly successful directory of Spanish-heritage librarians in the United States, *Quien Es Quien: A Who's Who of Spanish Heritage Librarians in the United States,* edited by Arnulfo Trejo, now retired from the University of Arizona School of Library Science.[3] This librarian survey and directory, now in its third edition, has been credited with focusing national attention on the need to train and hire greater numbers of Spanish-heritage librarians. It is hoped that the museum report and directory will have a similar impact with regard to Latino and Native American representation on museum professional staff.

QUANTITATIVE RESPONSE

The first phase of the survey project included a total of 2,000 questionnaires sent to 1,000 historical and 1,000 art museums. The total number of museums responding was 402, of which 227 were historical museums and 108 were art museums. A second mailing produced 67 additional responses: 28 from art museums and 39 from history museums. The mailing lists were obtained from the American Association of Museums. Latino and Native American institutions were identified from professional publications and other sources. As noted, the list of 2,000 institutions from the AAM targeted the top thousand historical and art museums in the United States in terms of funding levels of half a million dollars a year or more. The additional 400 museums include Latino and Native American institutions and other museums in areas of significant Latino and Native American populations. These were obtained mainly from other sources, including referrals from individual professionals. A follow-up mailing was sent to key institutions that did not respond to the first mailing of the survey. The second mailing focused on large to medium-sized museums in areas of high Latino and Native American populations, plus Latino and Native American museums that did not respond to the first mailing. A follow-up effort was also made to include additional biographical entries in the directory.

RESPONSES TO PART I

The analysis of responses to Part I obtained the following results. Answers to the question "How many of your professional staff members are Latinos?" totaled 52 for historical museums, 51 for art museums. Responses to the question "How many of your professional staff members are Native Americans?" totaled 47 for historical museums, 7 for art museums. Overall, there was a total of 104 Latino and 54 Native American museum professionals out of a total of 3,937 professional positions reported.

Responses to the question "How many professional museum staff members do you have in total?" indicated a total of 2,205 historical museum professional staff members and 1,732 art museum professional staff members. Responses to "How many of your Latino and Native American professional staff are women?" were 56 for historical museums and 31 for art museums. Responses to "How many of your professional staff are Mexican American?" totaled 36 for historical museums, and 22.5 for art museums (one response indicated one person as half Mexican American). To the question "How many of your professional staff are Puerto Rican?" historical museums responded 3, and art museums said 7. Responses to "How many of your professional staff are Cuban American?" were 4 for historical museums, 6 for art museums. Responses to "How many are from other Latin American nationalities?" totaled 9 for historical museums, 17 for art museums.

Another question asked, "How many are fluent Spanish speakers?/ How many are fluent speakers of a Native American Language?" Responses from historical museums indicated that 59 were fluent in Spanish and 27 in Native American languages, including 3 in Navajo, 2 in Mohawk, and 1 each in Cherokee, Oneida, and Crow. The others did not specify which languages. Responses from art museums indicated that 57 were fluent Spanish speakers, and one was fluent in Yucatec-Maya (Native American languages). To the question "How many members of your administrative professional staff are Latino and Native American?" historical museums replied that 23 were Latinos and 33 were Native Americans; art museums indicated that 27 were Latinos and 3 were Native Americans.

In answer to "How many members of your nonprofessional staff (maintenance, support, clerical) are Latino and Native American?" historical museums indicated that 126 Latinos and 26 Native Americans were nonprofessional employees, and art museums responded that 115 Latinos and 10 Native Americans were nonprofessionals. Responses to "How many are Latina and/or Native American women?" showed that 27 Latinas and 6 Native American women were nonprofessional employees in historical museums, and 43 Latina and 4 Native American women were nonprofessional employees in art museums.

QUALITATIVE RESPONSE

Qualitative evaluation of the responses suggests that while only limited observations can be made based on these data, it is clear that institutions and the profession as a whole have only begun to address the recruitment and training of Latino and Native American museum professionals. Despite the recommendations of "Museums for the New Century" and the increasing attention to diversity and multiculturalism at conferences and meetings and in publications and discussions, only a handful of institutions have initiated training programs for minorities, including Latinos and Native Americans. This positive, if limited, change sends a valuable message to the profession.

A few institutions stand out as models for the rest of the museum profession. One is the Museum of Fine Arts in Houston, which has hired significantly greater numbers of minority professional staff in comparison to similar institutions. It also operates a Minority Internship Program. Out of a total staff of fourteen at the Museum of Fine Arts, seven are Latino/a. Thus far, there are no Latino or Native American staff members among the collections/research staff. Another noteworthy effort is the Smithsonian Awards for Museum Leadership Program, focusing on museum professionals in all disciplines who are people of color. The program was created to foster career development and enhancement opportunities for such individuals. Begun at the time of the survey, the program appears to have had some impact on the careers of participants; one Latino participant, for example, is now executive director of a medium-sized regional history museum. This individual attributes the Smithsonian program with enhancing his professional skills, thus contributing to his effectiveness. A summer training workshop, the Latino Graduate Training Seminar (LGTS), began in the summer of 1994, developed by the Inter-University Program for Latino Research (IUP). Put on in conjunction with the Smithsonian, the seminar has begun to enhance that museum's diversity efforts (see "The National Latino Graduate Training Seminar" by E. Liane Hernandez).

Besides the summer seminar, the IUP has established a "Latinos in Museums" working group, based at the University of Arizona and Arizona State University.[4] In December 1993 a planning meeting of the working group took place at the Mexican Museum in San Francisco for the purpose of developing an agenda for research. Another important advance was the formation of a Latino Network and caucus within the American Association of Museums at its 1992 annual meeting. The AAM caucus was formed through the initiative of Latino professionals within the Smithsonian Museums.[5]

The National Association of Latino Arts and Culture (NALAC), formed in September 1992 at the National Association for Chicano Studies conference in San Antonio,[6] aims to influence public policy affecting Latinos in arts programs and museums. NALAC carried out research projects during 1994 and 1995 on the development of Latino museum and cultural programs (see "Chicano and Latino Art and Culture Institutions in the Southwest: The Politics of Space, Race, and Money" by Cynthia E. Orozco). The activities of this organization may have ramifications concerning issues of hiring, funding, and other key areas.

The Arizona State Museum at the University of Arizona has also initiated programs to assist and train Native American museum professionals.[7] The Arizona State Museum has also taken the lead in returning Native American religious and cultural artifacts and burial remains to Native American authorities. These efforts provide a significant model for other institutions in assisting the development of independent Native American museums and training of professionals.

During the study, visits were made to selected Latino institutions. Among these, notable examples of success are the Mexican Museum in San Francisco and the Mexican Fine Arts Center Museum of Chicago. The Mexican Fine Arts Center Museum has developed as the largest and strongest independent Latino museum in the nation.[8] It is located in a large renovated park building that has more than 15,000 square feet of floor space. There are three exhibit areas: the Main, West Wing, and Courtyard galleries. The West Wing gallery, which has a stage, also doubles as a performance area. The museum now has an annual budget in excess of $1 million, of which over 40 percent comes from public grants. Founded in 1982, the Mexican Fine Arts Center Museum has a Latino professional staff of ten, including a president, executive director, arts director, business director, development coordinator, permanent collections manager, arts education coordinator, performing arts coordinator, arts teacher, and permanent collections assistant. There are four other staff members: secretary, building custodian, gift shop assistant, and receptionist. The permanent collections include Graphic Art, Contemporary Art, Folk Art, and Photography. The Mexican Fine Arts Center Museum has developed outstanding educational and publications programs. The museum's more than twenty publications include high-quality catalogs with excellent color illustrations and text. It is particularly impressive that so many elementary and secondary school classes visit the museum, which hosts more than 900 docent-led tours each year.

The Mexican Museum in San Francisco counts two Latino staff members among its collections/research staff of six. All five of its programs staff members are Latino. Located at Fort Mason, the Mexican Museum has 8,800 square feet, including 3,129 square feet of gallery space. It has developed an impressive publications program, with over a dozen beautiful catalogs available. The museum has been especially effective in developing an excellent Mexican folk arts collection. A major construction campaign including a new building has been planned, with a projected construction cost of $11 million. When built, it will be the largest independent Latino museum in the nation.

Other, more recently established Latino museums include the MexicArte Museum in Austin, Texas,[9] and the Museo Chicano in Phoenix, Arizona, and the Museo de las Americas in Denver, Colorado. A more comprehensive study of independent Latino and Native American museums would yield valuable information concerning their development and operations and is clearly desirable at the present time.

FUTURE TRENDS AND ISSUES

Because the survey did obtain a favorable response from most of the large institutions contacted, it is possible to recognize some trends:

1. Although the museums and the museum profession have recognized the problem of representation of diversity, most of the emphasis has remained at the level of discussion.
2. A handful of institutions have initiated new programs to train and recruit staff from other ethnic groups besides Anglo-Americans.
3. An undetermined number of institutions have made few or token responses.
4. Some still deny the existence of a problem or the necessity for change in recruitment.

Existing efforts, while providing models, are inadequate to meet the needs of the nation's museums, the profession, and the public. Major efforts by the nation's museums will be required if diversity is to be achieved sometime during the first decades of the twenty-first century. Training and recruitment programs must be increased in number and quality and must be made effective in publicly supported museums. If affirmative action has resulted in minority access to representation in police, sanitation, and airport professions, it can and should also be extended to publicly funded museums.

Finally, it is recommended that research be carried out on critical issues regarding Latinos/as, their cultures, and their employment in museums. Such issues include the following:

1. The need for a larger, more comprehensive survey that would encompass all museums in the United States and Puerto Rico.
2. A historical and policy study of the development of independent Latino and Native American museums.
3. Studies of existing internships, summer seminars, and other training programs for Latino and Native American professionals.
4. A comprehensive study of the affirmative action process in public (city, county, state, and federal) institutions.
5. Studies of the effect of gender, cultural, language, and phenotypical bias in recruitment, advancement of Latinos/as, and Native Americans. Personnel interviews with Latino and Native American museum professionals suggest that gender bias, phenotype (skin color and other physical features), degree of acculturation, and accent are factors that selectively condition the recruitment, retention, and promotion of Latino and Native American museum professionals.
6. Studies of the effect of bias against ethnic history, ethnic studies, or women's studies in a backlash against Latino and Native American scholars trained in these disciplines.
7. The development and implementation of stronger national museum

policies that ensure equitable minority professional representation in public museums and that support Latino and Native American museums.

By focusing on those museums with a significant capability to impact Latino and Native American professional representation, the survey was able to initiate an assessment of these groups. The survey is intended to begin a process that will lead to a fully comprehensive national survey. It is hoped that the survey will bring national attention to the status of Latinos and Native Americans in the profession and that this attention will result in the hiring and training of individuals from these groups. For only by actively addressing this critical demand will the nation's museums be able to meet the needs of the twenty-first century.

ENDNOTES

1. The survey was developed and conducted by Antonio Ríos-Bustamante, assisted by research assistants Lillia Aguero and Elda Romero and staff editor Tom Gelsinon. The complete results of the survey have been published in Antonio Ríos-Bustamante, *Latinos and Native Americans in the Museum: The National Survey and Directory of Historical and Art Museum Professional Personnel* (Tucson: Mexican American Studies and Research Center, University of Arizona, 1996).

2. The literature concerning Latinos and Native Americans in museums or Latino museum programs include Marilyn Rose Guida, "A Contribution Toward Increasing Collaboration Between Museums and California Indians," *Western Museums Association News,* Spring 1996; Antonio Ríos-Bustamante, "El Orgullo De Ser: Latino Public History, Art and Museum Programs," Working Paper No. 17 (Tucson: Mexican American Studies and Research Center, University of Arizona, November 1990); Roberto Rodríguez, "Reclaiming History: Museum Survey Seeks to Increase Number of Latino and Native American Professionals," *Black Issues in Higher Education,* September 24, 1992; Veronica García and Toni Nelson Herrera, "Museums and Mexican Americans in Texas," *Musline,* Sept.-Oct. 1993, Texas Museum Association.

   Literature addressing lack of diversity includes the American Association of Museums (AAM) 1984 report, "Museums for the Next Century," in which the problem of non-Anglo-American representation among professional museum staff is underscored as a major challenge for the profession. Directing major efforts to remedy this problem was high on the report's list of recommendations. In 1989 the Ford Foundation released the report "Black and Hispanic Art Museums." Begun in 1986, this study reported on twenty-nine independent African American and Hispanic museums, which included the three major Latino museums: the Mexican Fine Arts Center Museum in Chicago, the Museo del Barrio in New York, and the Mexican

Museum in San Francisco. The first independent Latino museum in the United States was the Museo del Barrio, founded in 1969. A related report, titled "Cultural Centers of Color," was produced by the National Endowment for the Arts in 1992. This is a summary resulting from a study of 543 arts organizations. A profile section provides descriptions of selected organizations, including the Museo del Barrio and the Mexican Museum. In its 1992 report, "Excellence and Equity: Education and the Public Dimension of Museum," the AAM further recognized the need for changes to ensure that museums become more inclusive and pluralistic in their educational missions, serve more diverse audiences, and become more pluralistic workplaces. In chapter 8, it specifically calls for museums to "recruit and hire staff to reflect diversity at all levels in the museum."

3. Arnulfo D. Trejo (ed.), *Quien Es Quien: A Who's Who of Spanish-Speaking Librarians in the United States*, 4th ed. (Tucson: Hispanic Books Distributors and Publishers, 1986).

4. The IUP Working Group on Latinos in Museums is cochaired by the Antonio Ríos-Bustamante and Christine Marín of the Hayden Library at Arizona State University. The research agenda meeting was attended by fifteen Latino museum professionals, including representatives of three of the four major Latino museums and the American Association of Museums Latino Network.

5. The National Coordinator of the AAM Latino Network is Evelyn Figueroa, SITES Program, Smithsonian Traveling Exhibitions, 1100 Jefferson Dr. SW, Room 3146, Smithsonian Institution, Washington DC 20560, tel. (202) 357–2693.

6. The National Office of NALAC is located at 1300 Guadalupe Street, San Antonio, TX 78207–5519, tel. (210) 271–3151. National Chairperson is Juana Guzmán and Vice Chairperson is Pedro A. Rodríguez.

7. Raymond H. Thompson, "Looking to the Future: Museums Policy Shifts to the Issues of Control Over Heritage," *Museum News*, Jan.-Feb. 1991; John C. Ravesloot, "Communication and Cooperation Between the Arizona State Museum and Native Americans," *Museum Anthropology* 13, no. 3 (1989).

8. Mexican Fine Arts Center Museum, Report (Chicago, 1991).

9. Mexic-Arte has originated several significant touring exhibits, including "Contra Colonialismo," curated by Sylvia Orozco.

INDEX

DATE DUE

GAYLORD			PRINTED IN U.S.A.